THE EASIEST
ANTI-
INFLAMMATORY
COOKBOOK

FOR BEGINNERS
Restore Your Health and Relieve Persistent Pain
WITH SIMPLE RECIPES

Mary Anderson-Jones

IMPRINT

© 2024 TG Edition

1st edition

Author: Mary Anderson-Jones

Design: Linda Pixner

Cover design: Sprudelkopf Design | www.sprudelkoepfe.com

Cover image: iStockphotos © Plateresca

ISBN: 9791281216419

Publishing label: TG Edition

CONTACT

TG Edition

Thomas Larch

Feldbauernweg 22

39010 St. Martin in Passeier

Italy

E-Mail: support@tg-edition.com

IMAGE REFERENCE

S. 107: Alex9500 - Freepik; S. 106: zakiroff2000 - Freepik; S. 105: HandmadePictures - Freepik; S. 104: wirestock - Freepik; S. 103: Freepik - Freepik; S. 102: Freepik - Freepik; S. 101: rawpixel.com - Freepik; S. 98: EyeEm - Freepik; S. 95: KamranAydinov - Freepik; S. 95: Freepik - Freepik; S. 93: chandlervid85 - Freepik; S. 92: user20248055 - Freepik; S. 91: Freepik - Freepik; S. 90: lblinova - Freepik; S. 89: Freepik - Freepik; S. 86: Jcomp - Freepik; S. 84: devmaryna - Freepik; S. 73: KamranAydinov - Freepik; S. 72: KamranAydinov - Freepik; S. 70: 8photo - Freepik; S. 66: ismishko - Freepik; S. 66: timolina - Freepik; S. 64: Freepik - Freepik; S. 63: Freepik - Freepik; S. 62: All Item Stock - Freepik; S. 61: usinkovsa - Freepik; S. 60: Freepik - Freepik; S. 59: Freepik - Freepik; S. 57: EyeEm - Freepik; S. 56: topntp26 - Freepik; S. 55: Freepik - Freepik; S. 54: EyeEm - Freepik; S. 53: 8photo - Freepik; S. 52: timolina - Freepik; S. 50: sentavio - Freepik; S. 49: mjee7900 - Freepik; S. 48: Freepik - Freepik; S. 47: atlascompany - Freepik; S. 46: Freepik - Freepik; S. 45: Freepik - Freepik; S. 44: Freepik - Freepik; S. 43: stockking - Freepik; S. 42: venaki - Freepik; S. 41: yarunivstudio - Freepik; S. 38: nsit0108 - Freepik; S. 37: aleruana - Freepik; S. 34: Freepik - Freepik; S. 33: Freepik - Freepik; S. 32: Freepik - Freepik; S. 31: Racool_studio - Freepik; S. 30: ekaterinagay - Freepik; S. 29: EyeEm - Freepik; S. 28: Freepik - Freepik; S. 27: Racool_studio - Freepik; S. 26: wirestock - Freepik S. 24: pvproductions - Freepik; S. 17: Freepik - Freepik; S. 16: Drobotdean - Freepik; S. 15: Drazen Zigic - Freepik; S. 14: Freepik - Freepik; S. 13: drobotdean - Freepik; S. 12: Freepik - Freepik; S. 9: freepic.diller - Freepik; S. 7: undrey - Freepik; S. 6: Freepik - Freepik; S. 5: Freepik - Freepik; S. 4: Freepik - Freepik; S. 88: Olllympea - Depositphotos; S. 87: lenyvavsha - Depositphotos; S. 85: Anna_Shepulova - Depositphotos; S. 82: etorres69 - Depositphotos; S. 81: lenyvavsha - Depositphotos; S. 80: Magone - Depositphotos; S. 79: Brebca - Depositphotos; S. 78: homydesign - Depositphotos; S. 76: Rojoimages - Depositphotos; S. 75: Bhofack2 - Depositphotos; S. 74: Peteer - Depositphotos; S. 71: manera - Depositphotos; S. 68: minadezhda - Depositphotos; S. 67: duskbae - Depositphotos; S. 51: elenathewise - Depositphotos; S. 39: fotovincek - Depositphotos; S. 19: pinkasevich - Depositphotos;

DOWNLOAD YOUR FREE MEAL PLAN!

Thank you very much for your purchase.
Your decision to choose our book is greatly appreciated.

We are thrilled to offer you an exclusive bonus. Here, you'll find a complimentary 2-week meal plan and a customizable template to personalize your dietary journey. This way, it will be easier to maintain your healthy, anti-inflammatory lifestyle.

How to access the free content?
It's easy! Simply scan the QR code to download the meal plan directly from our website.

WE HOPE YOU ENJOY EXPLORING THESE NEW RECIPES AND INCORPORATING THEM INTO YOUR DAILY ROUTINE!

CONTENTS

FISH 52

VEGETARIAN VEGAN 62

SIDE DISHES
SAUCES 78

DESSERT 88

SNACKS 98

ANTI-INFLAMMATORY FOODS

Anti-inflammatory foods as the key to a healthy diet and a life with less pain.

We've all known for years that diet plays an important role in our health and well-being. What is not so well known, however, is the fact that we can also turn to foods that can prevent and fight inflammation in the body.

In a world where well-being is often compromised by stressful daily routines and unbalanced eating habits, anti-inflammatory nutrition offers a simple way to improve health and vitality. This cookbook is your key to a life full of energy, clarity, and enjoyment, free from the discomfort caused by chronic inflammation.

The anti-inflammatory diet is not just a way to relieve symptoms, but an invitation to experience the benefits of conscious eating. It promotes a stronger immune system, reduces the risk of chronic disease, and supports a holistic sense of well-being. By integrating the principles of this diet into your daily life, you are choosing to treat your body with love. Let's walk this path together and discover how delicious and enriching an anti-inflammatory diet can be.

In this cookbook, we will present tasty and healthy dishes and provide essential and helpful information on individual foods, their effects, and their processing. Anyone interested will have the opportunity to develop recipe ideas and put together their own menu tailored to their needs.

DISCOVER WITH US THE WORLD OF ANTI-INFLAMMATORY FOODS AND THE VARIETY THEY OFFER

———

Don't worry; we will explain a lot to you without turning it into a boring theory book. Because cooking and eating are pure pleasure - and an authentic experience if you can do it yourself.

WHAT IS INFLAMMATION?

WHAT CAUSES INFLAMMATION IN OUR BODY? WHAT ARE SIGNS OF INFLAMMATION IN OUR BODY?

Our diet directly **influences the health of one's body** and can also inhibit, alleviate, or ideally prevent inflammation. It is essential to eat the correct amount of the right foods and take specific complaints into account.

The motto of many people: "Losing weight always helps" is not true. However, it is true that being overweight promotes and supports numerous complaints, but **weight reduction alone is not a panacea.**

Inflammation in the body **can be triggered by** various factors, including **infections, injuries, and exposure to toxins**. Poor diet, stress, lack of exercise, and chronic conditions like obesity and autoimmune diseases can also contribute to inflammation. When the body detects **harmful stimuli, the immune system responds by releasing chemicals** that cause **blood vessels to leak fluid into tissues, leading to swelling and attracting white blood cells to the site of injury or infection**.

Signs of inflammation in the body **include redness, heat, swelling, pain,** and loss of function in the affected area. Chronic inflammation can manifest through persistent **fatigue, fever, mouth sores, rashes, abdominal pain, and chest pain**. Over time, unresolved inflammation can lead to more serious health issues such as **cardiovascular disease, diabetes, arthritis, and certain cancers**, highlighting the importance of managing and reducing inflammation through lifestyle and dietary choices.

WHAT DOES AN ANTI-INFLAMMATORY DIET DO TO OUR BODIES?

You can choose from a myriad of diets to lose weight. However, many of these diets only bring short-term success. They are designed to flush water out of the body but do not break down fat cells, for example. Subsequently, water is then stored again in these same fat cells. Within a short time, the success of the diet is often not maintained; this is known as **the "yo-yo effect".** Just like the popular children's toy, the weight goes up and down, up and down, up and down. Eventually, this is very frustrating - and promotes inflammation in the body.

A balanced diet is crucial, and not just when dieting. You should make sure that you get enough of all the vital nutrients. **This will also strengthen your immune system.** A body that is ideally nourished is strong and resilient. However, this only works if you change your diet permanently. This requires a lot of discipline. Fortunately, small "sins" are also allowed.

If you are struggling with inflammation, your diet is **an important step towards recovery.**

UNDER THE
SCIENTIFIC MICROSCOPE

Scientists have discovered that body fat promotes inflammation. Abdominal fat, in particular, stands out here. Therefore, obesity can be a root of evil.

Numerous products are constantly presented to us. They are always available to offer quick help when hungry. But this is precisely where the danger lies. Many of these products, whether fast food or sweets, contain saturated fats and **"empty" carbohydrates**. Saturated fats are solid fats at room temperature. In contrast, **liquid unsaturated fats** are considered healthier as **they help reduce the risk of heart disease** by increasing "good" HDL cholesterol levels and lowering "bad" LDL cholesterol levels.

"Empty" carbohydrates refer to foods mainly consisting of refined sugars and starches with

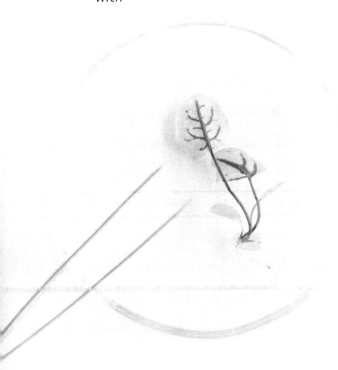

no significant nutritional value, such as vitamins, minerals, and fiber. They should be avoided wherever possible because they can lead to rapid fluctuations in blood sugar, which in the long term increases **the risk of type 2 diabetes**, obesity, and heart disease without providing the body with the necessary nutrients.

DIET HAS MANY EFFECTS ON OUR HEALTH, MAINLY THROUGH CERTAIN NUTRIENTS THAT CAN PROMOTE INFLAMMATION

Arachidonic acid, a fatty acid found primarily in animal products such as meat and sausage, as well as saturated fatty acids, is known to promote inflammatory processes by serving as a precursor for pro-inflammatory messengers. Animal proteins, cereals, and sweets can also promote inflammation by increasing acidity in the blood and tissues and sugar via hormonal pathways.

In contrast, **plants offer over 1000 substances with anti-inflammatory properties**. These plant substances can be found in various foods, such as vegetables, fruit, nuts, seeds, and whole-grains. We do not want to demonize the consumption of meat and animal products, as we also enjoy them. Instead, **our** focus is to emphasize the importance of a balanced and conscious diet, including fiber, which is essential for cell renewal.

When it comes to the fats naturally present in food, **you can make suitable adjustments to follow a healthier and anti-inflammatory diet**. Fish and nuts contain many omega-3 and omega-9 fatty acids, natural antagonists of arachidonic acid. A diet focusing on fruit, pulses, vegetables, nuts, and a few dairy products should be a sound basis for an anti-inflammatory diet.

According to medical experts, **a conscious and anti-inflammatory diet can be as effective as pain relief therapy with ibuprofen or diclofenac**. Despite all the differences in symptoms and causes, **the proper diet can have a very positive effect** on the body and alleviate and prevent inflammation in the body.

It is unnecessary to completely avoid carbohydrates, as they are essential to a balanced diet. But they should be the right carbohydrates. So, **choose whole-grain products if you want to eat a conscious and anti-inflammatory diet.** Whole-grain products are healthier because they contain more nutrients, fiber, and vitamins, aiding digestion and reducing the risk of heart disease and diabetes. You can cook or bake with **amaranth, millet, pulses, quinoa, or buckwheat** as an alternative to wheat and the gluten it contains. In addition to positively affecting joint and muscle pain or digestive problems, these ingredients also make a **tasty change** to your plate.

WITH THE RIGHT MIXTURE

You can alleviate your symptoms and perhaps even **get rid of them permanently without taking medication** or dietary supplements. That alone should be enough motivation to take a closer look at this topic.

You do not necessarily need to consult a medical specialist or an expensive dietitian. In general, an anti-inflammatory diet is an excellent start to reducing symptoms. However, ensure you consume all the nutrients the human body needs to function correctly.

UNDER THE
SCIENTIFIC MICROSCOPE

For a comprehensive and healthy diet, especially as part of an anti-inflammatory diet, the following nutrients should be consumed in sufficient quantities to provide the body with optimal nutrition:

1. ESSENTIAL FATTY ACIDS:
Omega-3 fatty acids, which are found in fish, flaxseed, chia seeds, and walnuts, are particularly important as they have anti-inflammatory properties.

2. PROTEINS:
For maintaining and repairing body tissues, lean protein sources such as poultry, fish, legumes, and nuts are preferable.

3. VITAMINS AND MINERALS:
Especially antioxidant vitamins such as vitamin C (in citrus fruits and peppers), vitamin E (in nuts and seeds), beta-carotene (in carrots and sweet potatoes), as well as the anti-inflammatory vitamin D (from sunlight exposure and in fatty fish) and zinc (in meat, shellfish and legumes).

4. DIETARY FIBER:
Important for digestion and to support a healthy microbiome; whole-grains, vegetables, fruits, and legumes are rich in fiber.

5. COMPLEX CARBOHYDRATES:
Instead of simple sugar sources, complex carbohydrates from whole-grain products, such as fruit and vegetables, should be preferred, as they ensure a long-lasting energy supply and help to avoid blood sugar peaks.

6. WATER AND FLUIDS:
Adequate fluid intake is essential for all bodily functions and supports the body's anti-inflammatory processes.

Together, these nutrients help the body function effectively, repair itself, and fight inflammation, which is essential for maintaining health and preventing disease.

A generally healthy lifestyle is at least as essential. The best medicine is a combination of a healthy diet, exercise, sufficient water, fresh air, and enough restful sleep.

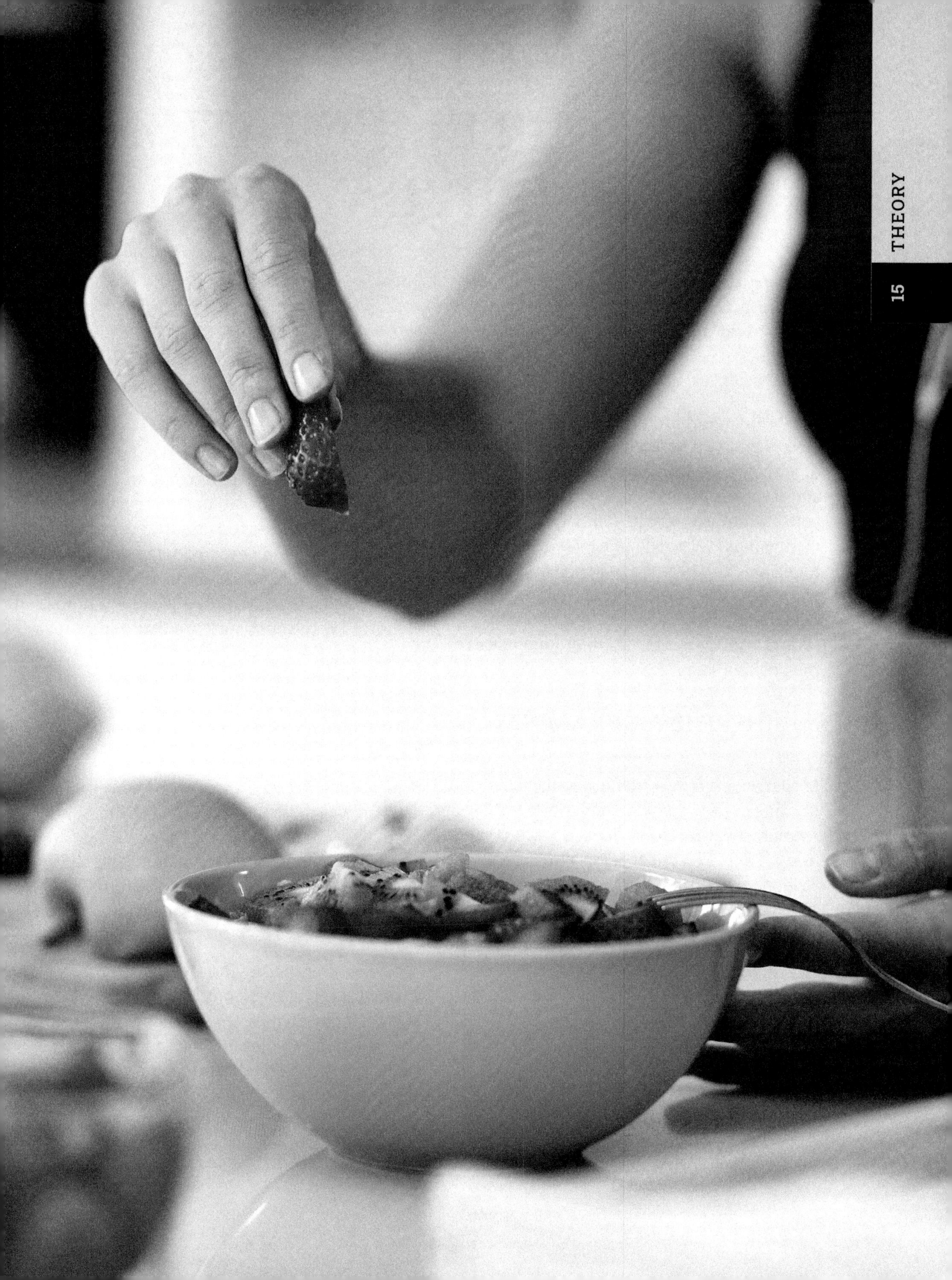

THE RIGHT APPROACH AND IMPLEMENTATION IN EVERYDAY LIFE

As with any innovation, it is crucial when introducing the anti-inflammatory diet not to rush into this phase unthinkingly and unprepared. Otherwise, it creates frustration when successes do not materialize at all or are soon undone. The dieter is dissatisfied and finds it difficult to try again.

Therefore, we will try to provide you with a kind of guide so that you can enter the world of anti-inflammatory nutrition in a structured and step-by-step manner. We will challenge you, but not overwhelm you. The magic word is "openness." Be open to new diets and foods, but also be open to yourself - and for yourself. Listen to your body, recognize its negative signals, and interpret them. You should also recognize, interpret, and react to the positive signs.

HERE IS AN EXAMPLE:
___

Sebastian is a family friend who has been complaining of joint pain for some time. His GP's recommendation to cut down on alcohol and lose weight fell on deaf ears: "I'm not going to let some health nut tell me how to live my life," was his credo.

We talked to him and managed to convince him to at least try it. He found it difficult at first. The schnitzel at lunchtime and the beer for dinner were too integrated into his regular routine. However, people find change difficult, and Sebastian was no exception. We accompanied him carefully and step-by-step. It started with shopping ("Are you kidding me? I can shop, I've been doing it for many years, I don't need you for that!"), continued with food preparation and, at some point, ended with Sebastian hardly drinking any alcohol of his own volition.

The journey we were allowed to take with Sebastian was more of a marathon than a short distance. And just like a marathon, Sebastian had to pace himself. A fundamental change in his entire lifestyle from one day to the next would most likely have been doomed to failure.

However, the successes that Sebastian was ultimately able to celebrate were overwhelming. He lost weight without feeling like he had to follow a strict diet. His joint pain decreased and almost completely disappeared, his complexion improved significantly, and he started to enjoy doing sports again, not just watching TV.

We can't accompany you quite as intensively as we did with Sebastian. However, you can still benefit from his and our experience.

DON'T RUSH INTO ANYTHING. APPROACH CHANGES CAUTIOUSLY

———

You can make this transition a little easier for yourself. Why not prepare a few vegetable sticks with a light dip for the evening on the PC or in front of the TV instead of snacking on sweets or processed snacks? You will see how varied and tasty this can be. Moreover, these small snacks are less of a burden on the body.

Ideally, you should avoid snacking in the evening altogether. Experts recommend not eating within three hours before bedtime. This is because the body digests much less well when you are asleep than when you are awake. Eating late at night can then result in sleep disorders and a tendency to put on weight. And you would have achieved the opposite of what you built up through discipline during the day.

Concentrate on eating several small meals rather than a few large meals. The effort your body puts into digesting the large meals will put additional strain on you. You will soon notice that you feel much more energetic than before.

Also, listen to your taste buds. No one is helped if you are reluctant to choke down your meals. Reducing some foods does not necessarily mean that you don't like your new diet.

Experts largely agree that red meat, for example, promotes rather than inhibits inflammation in the body. However, this does not mean you must go vegetarian or vegan - quite the opposite. Animal products contain a lot of protein, which the human body needs.

SO, AS WITH EVERYTHING IN LIFE, IT'S ALL ABOUT THE RIGHT MIX, ATTITUDE, AND PREPARATION

———

Let's look at what you should consider in preparation if you want to start with an anti-inflammatory diet.

STEP-BY-STEP TO AN ANTI-INFLAMMATORY DIET

Introducing an anti-inflammatory diet into your life should be a deliberate and gradual process that helps you establish long-term healthy habits without feeling overwhelmed. Here's a simple step-by-step guide to help you get started, even if you're a complete beginner:

1.

TAKE STOCK OF YOUR CURRENT DIET

Write down what you eat and drink for a week. Pay particular attention to how often fast food, processed foods, and pro-inflammatory foods such as sugar or white flour products are on your menu, as opposed to anti-inflammatory foods such as vegetables and whole-grains.

2.

REBUILD YOUR DIET

Analyze your records to see where changes are needed. Identify the foods that promote inflammation and consider healthier alternatives to replace them. Ask yourself questions like: What foods cause me problems? What healthy foods do I like, and how can I eat them more often?

This step-by-step approach allows you to make a stress-free transition to an anti-inflammatory diet that will help you feel healthier and improve your long-term well-being.

3.

CREATE A PLAN

——

Based on your inventory and identified problem areas, create a concrete plan for your meals and snacks. This plan should include easy, incremental changes that you can realistically implement. Aim to introduce more anti-inflammatory foods such as green leafy vegetables, berries, nuts, seeds, and fish rich in omega-3 fatty acids.

4.

IMPLEMENT THE 80/20 PRINCIPLE

——

Focus on choosing anti-inflammatory foods 80% of the time and allow yourself 20% of the time to be flexible. This approach prevents you from feeling overwhelmed or restricted. It helps you to integrate the new diet into your everyday life permanently. It's not about being perfect; it's about making conscious choices that benefit your health.

THE RIGHT PURCHASE

An anti-inflammatory diet does involve a change, but not necessarily horrendous costs or an insane amount of effort. Organic food is somewhat more expensive than conventionally produced goods. Fortunately, most supermarkets and discount stores also offer an affordable organic range. This ensures that healthy eating is not prohibitively expensive.

Conventional products can be an option when buying fruit and vegetables, especially if you pay attention to freshness and seasonality to benefit from an optimal nutrient content. However, **it is advisable to choose organic alternatives for products with a high pesticide load or to wash the food thoroughly and peel it if necessary.** This helps to reduce the intake of harmful residues.

For animal products, on the other hand, organic quality is an essential prerequisite for supporting a healthy diet. Conventional animal husbandry methods often involve using antibiotics and other medicines, which can adversely affect animals and humans, such as promoting antibiotic resistance. Organic-certified animal products are free from these additives, offer a higher content of essential nutrients such as omega-3 fatty acids, and ensure that animals are kept under more natural and species-appropriate conditions.

Consciously **choosing organic animal products promotes your health through higher quality food** and supports more sustainable and ethical farming.

BE SURE TO CHECK THE LIST OF INGREDIENTS IN READY MEALS

———

Most ready meals contain ingredients that hinder or at least make it more difficult to eat an anti-inflammatory diet. Make it easy for your body to fight inflammation by supporting it with the right foods. **The list of ingredients can be found on the back labels or on the sides of the products**. Allergens are highlighted in bold so that you can immediately see what you can and cannot eat if you suffer from one or more allergies.

We do not want to tell you what you can and cannot eat. To successfully tackle inflammation, it is also beneficial to feel good. And that works with food that you like. Even if you should or have to use some ingredients more sparingly.

An important tip: **never go shopping hungry**. This leads to careless purchases. You can also discipline yourself by **writing a shopping list based on your menu plan** and sticking to it meticulously. This will minimize the secret little emergency stocks of tasty but, unfortunately, absolutely unhealthy snacks and sweets in your home. However, you will find that you don't really miss those little treats at all.

SCAN FOR YOUR GROCERY LIST

WHICH FOODS SHOULD I AVOID, IF POSSIBLE?

To implement the anti-inflammatory diet, minimizing some factors jeopardizing success is important.

Some people will find it challenging to cut out **fast food**. But as temptingly easy as it is to get hold of these foods, they are **usually unhealthy**. Saturated **fatty acids** and **white flour** with no content and **flavor enhancers** put unnecessary strain on you. **Fast food should be better avoided if you are dealing with inflammation in your body.** Look for healthier alternatives!

Highly processed foods

Dairy products only in moderation

White flour products

Coffee on an empty stomach

Sugar

Found in some margarine

Trans fats

Ready meals

Avoid these foods as much as possible

Soft drinks

Baked goods

Salt products

Red meat

Potato chips

Peanut flips

Sausage

Alcohol

Salt sticks

THE REVERSE CONCLUSION: WHAT SHOULD I EAT?

There are, of course, safe foods that form the basis of an anti-inflammatory diet. Depending on the type of complaint and the cause of the inflammation in the body, these foods include:

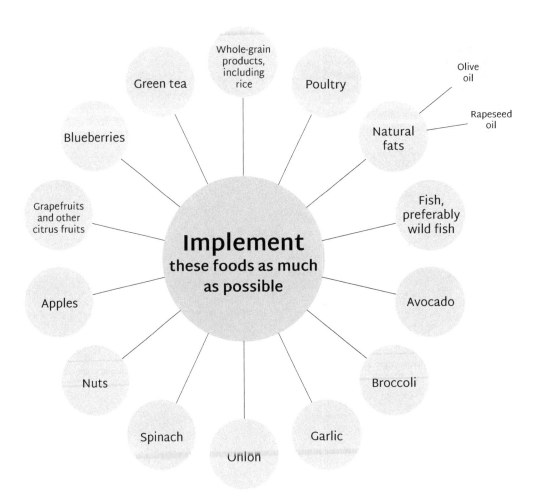

Green tea

Whole-grain products, including rice

Poultry

Olive oil

Blueberries

Natural fats

Rapeseed oil

Grapefruits and other citrus fruits

Fish, preferably wild fish

Implement these foods as much as possible

Apples

Avocado

Nuts

Broccoli

Spinach

Garlic

Onion

BUT YOU SHOULD BE ABLE TO FEEL GOOD

Just as important as food is the lifestyle itself. You have probably already heard the term "work-life balance." This term describes the balance between work and private life. Both are part of a healthy lifestyle, but they should also be in reasonable proportion. Try to structure your day well: Work, leisure, and sleep should ideally occur in equal proportions.

Pay attention to what you eat and make sure your diet is **balanced and nutritious**. Take precedence over supplements, which only serve as an addition to a balanced diet. Not all supplements are problematic; the key is to check carefully which ones you are taking and the ingredients carefully. The aim should be to get the nutrients you need mainly from **natural foods** and only use supplements as an add-on to support your diet when needed.

"MENS SANA IN CORPORE SANO"

————

Translated, this saying means something like: **"In a healthy body, there is a healthy mind."** As with many sayings, there is an undeniable kernel of truth here, as a body that is at peace with itself will not distract your mind with trivial matters, such as the perception of inflammatory pain. Simply because these pains are not there. And it's as simple as it sounds. The sublime feeling of being exhausted but also proud and happy after a strenuous sports session more than makes up for all the effort.

Let's briefly summarize once again: **You should avoid stress, alcohol, fatty and too-rich food, sugar, snacks, too much salt, white flour products, and red meat as well as coffee on an empty stomach** as much as possible so as not to put too much strain on your body and overload your digestion.

On the other hand, you will be doing yourself and your body a huge favor if you **ensure you get enough sleep, avoid stress, eat fresh vegetables, exercise, and drink suitable beverages**. Green tea is particularly recommended.

If you sometimes find it difficult to stick to your diet plan, this is not at all dramatic. In nutritional science, there is the Pareto principle. You've never heard of it? Basically, it's about achieving an **80/20 ratio**. In concrete terms, this means that **80% of your diet should focus on anti-inflammatory foods, and 20% can be foods you simply enjoy**. This makes it easier for you to change your diet permanently. On the other hand, it prevents chocolate cravings, for example, which can occur if you have to go without it for a long time and under duress.

FAQ

THE MOST

PRESSING QUESTIONS

ARE DAIRY PRODUCTS ALLOWED?

The anti-inflammatory diet is not about bans but about a conscious diet. Although dairy products are not harmless, they are okay in moderation. Of course, no general answer exists to how much you can tolerate and consume. In an anti-inflammatory diet, dairy products can be consumed in moderation, depending on individual tolerance and the body's reaction. Some people tolerate dairy products well and can benefit from the nutrients they contain, such as calcium and protein. Others may be sensitive to specific components in dairy products, such as lactose or certain milk proteins, which can cause inflammatory reactions. Fermented dairy products such as yogurt, kefir, or certain cheeses are often better tolerated. They can even positively affect intestinal health, which can have an anti-inflammatory effect. The rule here is: the proof of the pudding is in the eating!

DO YOU HAVE TO GIVE UP GLUTEN COMPLETELY?

Here, too, it's more about conscious nutrition than bans. Although gluten is not the ideal accompaniment to an anti-inflammatory diet, it is very rarely necessary to give it up completely.

HOW QUICKLY CAN YOU SEE THE RESULTS?

It is very difficult to give a general answer. It always depends on your goal and where you are starting from. You will quickly notice the first results if you want to lose weight. With other dietary changes aimed directly at inflammation, it may take some time to see lasting results. However, when these results occur, your quality of life will improve dramatically! Don't worry; it won't take years to see the results.

SHOULD I AVOID NIGHTSHADE PLANTS? (POTATO, TOMATO...)

Nightshades are a family of plants (Solanaceae), including popular vegetables such as tomatoes, potatoes, peppers, and eggplants. In principle, you can also eat nightshade plants without hesitation. However, the correct preparation is essential. If you want to fry or roast potatoes, this is not ideal. Boiled potatoes, on the other hand, are no problem. You can enjoy tomatoes anyway; they are a source of vitamins and don't strain you or your body too much.

HOW IMPORTANT IS FLUID INTAKE WITH THIS DIET?

Fluid intake is of central importance. You should mainly drink water and green tea, but soft drinks and especially alcohol should be consumed very sparingly.

WHAT SHOULD I BEAR IN MIND WHEN EATING IN A RESTAURANT?

Try to find something that supports your anti-inflammatory diet. However, it is not a huge problem if this is not possible. The anti-inflammatory diet is not a religion. Remember the Pareto principle: 80% of your diet should focus on anti-inflammatory foods, and 20% can be foods you simply enjoy.
So, if you eat consciously, you can be a little more lax if there are exceptions.

WILL THE ANTI-INFLAMMATORY DIET ALSO HELP ME IF I HAVE ALLERGIES?

Even people with allergies can follow an anti-inflammatory diet without any problems. It can become difficult with allergies that affect the more favorable foods. If you are allergic to certain nuts, consider the ingredients when shopping. Allergenic substances must be labeled by law.

This type of diet can even have a lasting beneficial effect on your allergy. Just as allergies can be acquired and aggravated by environmental influences, lifestyle, and diet, they can also be alleviated with the appropriate measures.

BREAKFAST

BERRY AND SPINACH SMOOTHIE

| Easy | Glass | 10 Minutes | Vegan | Gluten-free | Nut-free |

INGREDIENTS

1 cup	mixed berries (fresh or frozen, e.g., strawberries, blueberries, raspberries)
1	ripe banana
½	avocado
2 tbsp	chia seeds

1 cup	almond milk (or other plant milk of your choice)
1 tsp	fresh ginger, peeled and grated

1 handful of fresh spinach

Optional: 1 tsp turmeric powder for additional anti-inflammatory effect, Ice cubes (as required)

PREPARATION

1. Place the berries in the blender together with the peeled banana.

2. Add fresh spinach and halved, pitted avocado.

3. Add the chia seeds, grated ginger, and optional turmeric powder to the blender.

4. Add the almond milk and ice cubes, if using.

5. Blend everything to a smooth and creamy consistency.

6. Pour the smoothie into a large glass and serve.

Nutritional information (per serving)
Calories 350 kcal; Protein 6 g; Fat 15 g;
Sugar 25 g; Carbohydrates 50 g

CARROT AND GINGER SMOOTHIE

 Easy   **Glass**   **10 Minutes**   **Vegan**   **Gluten-free**   **Nut-free**

INGREDIENTS

2	carrots, peeled and roughly chopped	**¾ cups**	coconut water
1	apple, cored and roughly chopped	**1 tbsp**	linseed
½	ripe banana	**1 tsp**	turmeric powder
¾ inch	fresh ginger, peeled		

A pinch of black pepper (to improve the absorption of curcumin)

Optional: Ice cubes

PREPARATION

1. Place the carrots, apple, banana, and ginger in a high-powered blender.

2. Add coconut water to lighten the mixture and achieve a smooth consistency

3. Add linseed, turmeric powder, and a pinch of black pepper to the blender

4. Optionally add ice cubes if a cooler version of the smoothie is desired.

5. Blend everything at high speed until the smoothie is completely smooth.

6. Pour the smoothie into a large glass and serve immediately.

Nutritional information (per serving)
Calories 180 kcal; Protein 2 g; Fat 1 g;
Sugar 15 g; Carbohydrates 40 g

CUSTOMIZE SMOOTHIE ACCORDING TO PREFERENCE:

Smoothies can easily be adapted to personal preferences and nutritional needs by combining different ingredients. It is important to always include a base of anti-inflammatory components such as leafy greens (e.g., spinach or kale), healthy fats (e.g., avocado or chia seeds), and a source of antioxidants (e.g., berries or turmeric). Bananas or mangoes can be added for extra sweetness and creaminess. At the same time, plant milk or coconut water provides a liquid base. This flexible approach ensures the smoothie remains delicious, nutrient-rich, and anti-inflammatory.

AVOCADO AND EGG TOAST

Easy   **Serving**   **15 Minutes**   **Vegetarian**   **Lactose-free**   **Gluten-free (optional)**

INGREDIENTS

2 slices of wholemeal bread (choose gluten-free bread for a gluten-free version)

1 ripe avocado

2 eggs

1 tsp olive oil

A few leaves of fresh spinach or rocket

Optional: A squeeze of lemon juice and a few chili flakes for extra flavor

PREPARATION

1. Place the wholemeal bread in the toaster and toast as desired.

2. Halve the avocado, remove the pit, and mash the flesh in a bowl with a fork.

3. Heat the olive oil in a pan and cook the eggs as fried or poached as desired.

4. Place the toasted bread on a plate, spread with the mashed avocado, and sprinkle with a pinch of sea salt and freshly ground black pepper.

5. Carefully place the eggs on the avocado-covered toast.

6. Garnish with fresh spinach leaves or rocket, and optionally sprinkle with a squeeze of lemon juice and chili flakes.

Nutritional information (per portion)
Calories 400 kcal; Protein 14 g; Fat 30 g;
Sugar 4 g; Carbohydrates 30 g

AVOCADO

———

The avocado is a true superhero among foods. Rich in monounsaturated fats, it provides a wealth of nutrients, including vitamin K, vitamin E, folic acid, and potassium - even more than a banana! This creamy fruit is rich in fiber, which aids digestion and also provides long-lasting satiety. Ideally, you should eat 2–3 avocados a week to reap the benefits. Compared to other foods, avocados are high in antioxidants and anti-inflammatory properties, which help to protect the body from free radicals and reduce inflammation. So not only does the avocado support a healthy heart, but it can also reduce the risk of certain diseases and contribute to general well-being.

HOMEMADE PEANUT BUTTER

 Easy   **Glasses** (2)   **15 Minutes**   **Vegan**   **Gluten-free**

INGREDIENTS

2 cups	unsalted, roasted peanuts
2 tbsp	extra virgin olive oil or coconut oil
1 tsp	turmeric powder
½ tsp	ground cinnamon
	A pinch of ground ginger
	Optional: A pinch of salt

PREPARATION

1. Place the peanuts in a high-powered blender or food processor. Blend or pulse on high speed until the peanuts begin to form a paste. This may take a few minutes. Scrape down the sides of the container if necessary.

2. Add olive or coconut oil, turmeric powder, cinnamon, ginger, and salt (if using) to the ground peanuts.

3. Continue blending until the mixture is smooth and creamy. You can add more oil depending on the desired consistency. For a creamier peanut butter, stir in a little more oil. For a firmer consistency, use less.

4. Taste the peanut butter and adjust the seasoning to your taste. If you like it sweeter, you could add a teaspoon of honey or maple syrup, but be aware that this could affect the anti-inflammatory properties.

5. Transfer the peanut butter to a clean jar with a tight-fitting lid. Store in the refrigerator and consume within one month.

Nutritional information (per tablespoon)
Calories 100 kcal; Protein 4 g; Fat 8 g; Sugar 4 g; Carbohydrates 3 g

NUTS

Nuts are full of nutrients and play an essential role in a balanced diet. They provide high-quality unsaturated fats, proteins, fiber, vitamins, and minerals such as vitamin E, magnesium, and selenium, which contribute to heart health, improve cholesterol levels, and support metabolism. The difference between the nut types lies in their specific nutrient profile; walnuts are rich in omega-3 fatty acids, while almonds are exceptionally high in vitamin E. Nutrition experts consider walnuts to be particularly healthy due to their high content of omega-3 fatty acids. Eating a small handful of nuts daily is recommended. Nuts support an anti-inflammatory diet due to their antioxidant and healthy fat content, which can help reduce inflammation and the risk of chronic disease.

SEEDS

Seeds, such as chia, linseed, and pumpkin, are real nutrient bombs that enrich any diet. They provide high-quality omega-3 fatty acids, fiber, protein, and essential micronutrients. These little powerhouses support heart health and digestion and have an anti-inflammatory effect, making them an important part of an anti-inflammatory diet. Regular consumption of seeds can help to reduce inflammation in the body and promote overall well-being. Their versatility makes them an easy addition to any meal, whether sprinkled over morning yogurt, blended into smoothies, or as a crunchy topping on salads.

MANGO-COCONUT-CHIA PUDDING

 Easy

 4 Glasses

 15 Minutes
+ overnight soaking

 Vegan

 Gluten-free

 Nut-free

INGREDIENTS

1   ripe mango

1 ⅔ cups coconut milk

¼ cup   chia seeds

1 tsp   vanilla extract

Sea salt

Optional: 1 tbsp maple syrup (depending on desired sweetness), a few fresh berries and mint leaves for decoration

PREPARATION

1. Peel the mango and separate the flesh from the stone. Then, cut the flesh into pieces.

2. Finely purée half of the mango pieces in a blender with the coconut milk, maple syrup, vanilla extract, and a pinch of sea salt.

3. Stir the chia seeds into the mango and coconut mixture.

4. Pour the mixture into bowls or glasses and top with the remaining mango pieces.

5. Leave the pudding in the fridge overnight so that the chia seeds swell and form a pudding-like consistency.

6. Before serving, the pudding can be decorated with fresh berries and mint leaves.

Nutritional information (per portion)
Calories 320 kcal; Protein 5 g; Fat 20 g;
Sugar 15 g; Carbohydrates 25 g

SUGAR-FREE GRANOLA

 Easy
 Portions
 10 Minutes
 Vegan
 Gluten-free
 Nut-free

INGREDIENTS

2 cups	gluten-free rolled oats	1 tsp	cinnamon
½ cup	pumpkin seeds	1 tsp	vanilla extract
½ cup	sunflower seeds	½ cup	unsweetened shredded coconut
¼ cup	linseed	½ cup	dried berries (e.g., blueberries or cranberries), unsweetened
¼ cup	chia seeds		
2 tbsp	coconut oil, melted		Sea salt
¼ cup	maple syrup		

PREPARATION

1. Preheat the oven to 320 °F (160 °C) and line a tray with baking paper.

2. Mix the oats, pumpkin, sunflower, linseed, and chia seeds in a large bowl.

3. Add the melted coconut oil, maple syrup, cinnamon, vanilla extract, and a pinch of sea salt, stirring well until everything is evenly moistened.

4. Spread the mixture evenly on the prepared baking sheet and bake for about 20 minutes, until the granola is golden brown and crispy. Stir once halfway through to ensure even browning.

5. Remove the granola from the oven and leave to cool. Once cool, mix in the shredded coconut and dried berries.

6. Store the cooled granola in an airtight container.

Nutritional information (per serving)
Calories 200 kcal; Protein 6 g; Fat 10 g; Sugar 5 g; Carbohydrates 24 g

THREE REASONS WHY YOU SHOULD AVOID INDUSTRIALLY PRODUCED SUGAR

---

1. Health: Avoiding industrial sugar can reduce the risk of chronic diseases such as diabetes, heart disease, and certain cancers.

2. Healthy balance: High-sugar foods are often high in calories and low in nutrients, which can lead to weight gain. Without industrial sugar, it's easier to maintain a healthy balance.

3. Well-being: Cutting out sugar can lead to more stable blood sugar levels, which reduces fluctuations in energy and mood and improves overall well-being.

GRAIN BREAD

WITH NUTS

 Medium Bread 1 Hour 15 Minuters incl. baking time Vegan Gluten-free

INGREDIENTS

1 ¾ cups	buckwheat flour	½ tsp	baking powder (gluten-free)
1 cup	ground almonds	2 cups	water
1 ¾ oz	sunflower seeds	2 tbsp	extra virgin olive oil
1 ¾ oz	pumpkin seeds	Sea salt	
2 tbsp	chia seeds		
2 tbsp	linseed		
2 tbsp	psyllium husks		

Optional: A handful of walnuts, roughly chopped

PREPARATION

1. Preheat the oven to 360 °F (180 °C) and line a loaf tin with baking paper or grease with olive oil.

2. In a large bowl, mix the buckwheat flour, ground almonds, sunflower seeds, pumpkin seeds, chia seeds, linseed, psyllium husks, sea salt, and baking powder.

3. Add the water and olive oil and mix everything into a smooth batter. Fold in the walnuts if using.

4. Pour the batter into the prepared loaf tin and smooth the surface.

5. Bake the bread in the preheated oven for about 60 minutes, until it has a golden brown crust and a wooden skewer inserted into the center comes out clean.

6. Remove the bread from the oven and leave to cool in the tin for 10 minutes. Then, leave to cool completely on a cooling rack.

Nutritional information (per portion)
Calories 280 kcal; Protein 8 g; Fat 18 g;
Sugar 1 g; Carbohydrates 24 g

GLUTEN-FREE BREAD

 Medium   **Bread**   **1 Hour 20 Minutes** incl. baking & resting time   **Vegan**   **Gluten-free**

INGREDIENTS

2 cups	gluten-free flour (e.g., buckwheat flour or a gluten-free flour blend)
1 cup	ground linseed
½ cup	chia seeds
1 tsp	baking powder (gluten-free)
2 tbsp	apple cider vinegar

1 ½	cups water
2 tbsp	extra virgin olive oil
Sea salt	

Optional: 1/2 cup pumpkin seeds or sunflower seeds for the filling

PREPARATION

1. Preheat the oven to 360 °F (180 °C) and line a loaf tin with baking paper or grease with a little olive oil.

2. Mix gluten-free flour, ground linseed, chia seeds, sea salt, and baking powder in a large bowl.

3. Add the apple cider vinegar, water, and olive oil and mix everything into a smooth batter.

4. If desired, work pumpkin seeds or sunflower seeds into the batter.

5. Pour the batter into the prepared loaf tin and smooth the surface.

6. Bake the bread in the preheated oven for about 60 minutes until it is golden brown and a wooden skewer inserted into the center comes out clean.

7. Remove the bread from the oven and leave to cool in the tin for 10 minutes. Then, leave to cool completely on a cooling rack.

Nutritional information (per portion)
Calories 180 kcal; Protein 5 g; Fat 9 g; Sugar 0 g; Carbohydrates 20 g

GLUTEN-FREE

———

A gluten-free diet is particularly essential for people with coeliac disease or gluten intolerance, as gluten can lead to inflammation and damage to the digestive tract in these cases. However, people without these diagnoses also report improved well-being without gluten, as it can reduce digestive problems and inflammatory processes. The difference between gluten-containing and gluten-free foods lies in the absence of gluten proteins in the latter, which can be important in an anti-inflammatory diet to minimize inflammatory reactions in the body. Thus, eliminating gluten not only supports intestinal health but can also help to reduce inflammation in general.

BERRIES

Berries play a central role in the anti-inflammatory diet because they are rich in antioxidants, especially anthocyanins, which give them their bright colors and help reduce inflammation in the body. These powerful plant compounds help to strengthen the immune system, reducing the risk of many chronic diseases. Berries also provide important vitamins and minerals that promote overall health and well-being. Their fiber also helps improve gut health and plays a role in maintaining a healthy body weight, which can also help lower inflammatory markers.

ALMOND YOGURT

WITH BERRIES AND GRANOLA

| Easy | Portion | 10 Minutes | Vegan | Gluten-free |

INGREDIENTS

. . . .

7 oz almond yogurt (unsweetened)

1 ¾ oz homemade granola according to our recipe

1 tbsp chia seeds

1 handful of fresh berries (e.g., blueberries, strawberries, raspberries)

Optional: 1 tsp honey or maple syrup for extra sweetness

PREPARATION

. . . .

1. Place the almond yogurt in a bowl.

2. Wash the fresh berries and half, or leave them whole as required. Sprinkle over the yogurt.

3. Spread the homemade granola evenly over the berries.

4. Sprinkle chia seeds on top to add extra omega-3 fatty acids and fiber.

5. Optionally sweeten with a teaspoon of honey or maple syrup if a sweeter taste is desired.

6. Stir briefly before eating to blend all layers.

Nutritional information (per portion)
Calories 300 kcal; Protein 8 g; Fat 15 g;
Sugar 10 g; Carbohydrates 35 g

OVERNIGHT OATS

Easy

Glass

5 Minutes & overnight

Vegan

INGREDIENTS

⅓ cup	gluten-free rolled oats
1 cup	almond milk or another plant based milk of your choice
1 tbsp	chia seeds
½ tsp	turmeric powder
¼ tsp	cinnamon
1 tbsp	maple syrup or honey (for a vegan version, use maple syrup)

A pinch of black pepper (to improve the absorption of curcumin)

Fresh berries or mango for the topping

Optional: 1 tbsp ground flax-seed for extra omega-3 fatty acids

PREPARATION

1. Combine the rolled oats, chia seeds, turmeric powder, cinnamon, a pinch of black pepper, and optional ground flax seeds in a bowl or Mason jar.

2. Add the almond milk and maple syrup (or honey) and stir well until the ingredients are evenly distributed.

3. Cover the mixture and leave to soak in the fridge overnight, at least 8 hours, to achieve a creamy consistency.

4. Stir before serving and add a little more plant milk if necessary to achieve the desired consistency.

5. Garnish with fresh berries or mango pieces and serve.

Nutritional information (per serving)
Calories 320 kcal; Protein 9 g; Fat 8 g; Sugar 12 g; Carbohydrates 52 g

COMBINATIONS
—

For an anti-inflammatory effect, choose additions such as chia seeds, flax seeds, berries, nuts, and spices such as cinnamon or turmeric. Make sure to use natural sweeteners such as honey or maple syrup sparingly. There are many possible combinations, from fresh fruit and nut butter to cocoa for chocolate lovers. When putting together your overnight oats, make sure you have a balanced mix of complex carbohydrates, healthy fats, and proteins to provide energy for the day and reduce inflammation in the body.

OAT PORRIDGE

| Easy | Portions | 15 Minutes | Vegan |

INGREDIENTS

80 g	rolled oats	**2 tbsp**	raisins or dried cranberries
400 ml	almond milk or another plant-based milk of your choice	**1 tbsp**	maple syrup or honey
1 tsp	cinnamon		A pinch of sea salt
½ tsp	ginger powder		Fresh fruit to garnish, such as berries or apple pieces
1 tbsp	linseed		

MILK ALTERNATIVES

In an anti-inflammatory diet, dairy alternatives such as almond milk, oat milk, and coconut milk play a key role as they contain natural, plant-based fats and nutrients that can reduce inflammation in the body. Unlike cow's milk, which can trigger inflammation and digestive discomfort in some people, these alternatives offer an easily digestible and low-allergen option. They are rich in vitamins, minerals, and antioxidants, support a healthy cardiovascular system, and contribute to overall health. Therefore, switching to dairy alternatives can positively reduce inflammation and promote a healthy lifestyle.

PREPARATION

1. Place the rolled oats and almond milk in a saucepan and bring to a boil over medium heat.

2. Add the cinnamon, ginger powder, and a pinch of sea salt and stir well.

3. Reduce the heat and simmer the porridge for about 10 minutes, stirring occasionally, until it has reached a creamy consistency.

4. Stir in the flaxseed, raisins (or cranberries), and maple syrup (or honey) and simmer for 2 additional minutes.

5. Remove the porridge from the heat and pour into bowls.

6. Garnish with fresh fruit.

Nutritional information (per portion)
Calories 300 kcal; Protein 7 g; Fat 7 g;
Sugar 15 g; Carbohydrates 50 g

PUMPKIN AND CINNAMON PORRIDGE

Easy | **Portions** 2 | **25 Minutes** & time for preparing the pumpkin purée | **Vegan** | **Gluten-free**

INGREDIENTS

7 oz	pumpkin purée
¾ cups	almond milk or another plant-based milk of your choice
1 ¾ oz	quinoa, well rinsed
1 tsp	cinnamon
½ tsp	ground ginger

¼ tsp	ground nutmeg
1 tbsp	maple syrup or honey
Sea salt	

Optional: 1 tbsp chia seeds for extra omega-3 fatty acids and fiber

PREPARATION

1. Cut a medium-sized pumpkin (e.g., Hokkaido or butternut) in half and remove the seeds. Place the halves cut-side down on a baking tray lined with baking paper.

2. Bake in a preheated oven at 360 °F (180 °C) for about 40–50 minutes until the pumpkin flesh is soft.

3. Remove the pumpkin from the oven, leave it to cool slightly, and then remove the soft flesh from the skin with a spoon.

4. Place the pumpkin flesh in a blender and purée until smooth. Excess water can be poured off if necessary to achieve the desired consistency.

Continue with the preparation of the porridge:

5. In a medium saucepan, bring the almond milk to a boil along with the quinoa.

6. Add the cinnamon, ginger, nutmeg, maple syrup (or honey), and a pinch of sea salt. Stir everything well.

7. Reduce the heat and simmer the porridge for about 15 minutes, stirring occasionally, until the quinoa is soft and most of the liquid has been absorbed.

8. Stir in the homemade pumpkin purée and continue to simmer until the porridge reaches a creamy consistency. Optionally, add the chia seeds and stir well.

9. Remove the finished porridge from the heat and pour into bowls.

10. Serve warm and garnish with a drizzle of maple syrup, a pinch of cinnamon, or fresh fruit, if desired.

Nutritional information (per serving)
Calories 250 kcal; Protein 7 g; Fat 5 g; Sugar 10 g; Carbohydrates 45 g

PUMPKIN

Pumpkin is a true superfood in the anti-inflammatory diet, thanks to its high levels of beta-carotene and other antioxidants that protect the body from harmful free radicals. These nutrients help to reduce inflammation and strengthen the immune system. Pumpkin is also rich in vitamins C and E, potassium, and fiber, promoting heart health and aiding digestion.

SPINACH PANCAKES

 Medium   **Portions** 4   **40 Minutes**   **Vegetarian**   **Gluten-free**   **Lactose-free**

BREAKFAST

A balanced breakfast is essential in an anti-inflammatory diet to provide the body with anti-inflammatory nutrients first thing in the morning and stabilize energy levels. It supports the body's defense against inflammation and promotes general health. On the other hand, skipping breakfast can lead to cravings and suboptimal eating choices that can promote inflammation. An anti-inflammatory breakfast should include complex carbohydrates, proteins, and healthy fats, such as oatmeal with nuts and berries or avocado and egg toast.

INGREDIENTS

5 oz	sourdough (gluten-free, if necessary)
3.5 oz	buckwheat flour or other gluten-free flour
1 cup	almond milk or another plant-based milk of your choice
1 tbsp	extra virgin olive oil, plus a little more for frying
1	large organic egg, beaten
7 oz	fresh spinach, washed
1	medium red onion, finely chopped
2	cloves of garlic, finely chopped

Sea salt

Freshly ground black pepper to taste

Optional: 1 tsp turmeric powder for additional anti-inflammatory properties

PREPARATION

1. Mix the sourdough, buckwheat flour, almond milk, 1 tbsp olive oil, sea salt, and black pepper in a large bowl to form a smooth dough.

2. Fold the beaten egg into the batter until fully incorporated. Optionally, add turmeric powder for additional anti-inflammatory benefits.

3. Heat some olive oil in a large frying pan over medium heat. Add the red onion, garlic, and sauté for 2–3 minutes until soft.

4. Add the spinach and sauté until wilted. Remove the spinach mixture from the pan and set aside.

5. Heat the pan again with a bit of olive oil. For each pancake, pour about a ladle-ful of the batter into the pan and smooth it out to form a round shape. Fry over medium heat until golden brown on both sides.

6. Place the finished pancakes on a plate and fill or arrange the spinach mixture on top.

Nutritional information (per portion)
Calories 220 kcal; Protein 6 g; Fat 10 g;
Sugar 2 g; Carbohydrates 28 g

SCRAMBLED EGGS
WITH MUSHROOMS

 Easy   Portions   25 Minutes   Vegetarian   Gluten-free   Lactose-free

INGREDIENTS

4	eggs	½ tsp	turmeric powder
7 oz	mushrooms, sliced	Sea salt	
1 tbsp	olive oil	Freshly ground black pepper	
1	onion, finely diced		
2 tbsp	parsley, chopped	**Optional:** 1 tsp linseed oil for garnish	

PREPARATION

1. Heat the olive oil in a frying pan over medium heat. Add the diced onion and fry for 2–3 minutes until translucent.

2. Add the mushroom slices to the onions and fry for 5–7 minutes until soft and lightly browned.

3. In a bowl, whisk the eggs with the turmeric powder, sea salt, and black pepper. Add the eggs to the mushrooms and onions in the pan.

4. Allow the eggs to set over low to medium heat, stirring constantly, until the scrambled eggs reach the desired consistency.

5. Remove the scrambled eggs from the heat and garnish with fresh parsley (and optional linseed oil).

6. Serve immediately.

Nutritional information (per portion)
Calories 250 kcal; Protein 7 g; Fat 5 g;
Sugar 10 g; Carbohydrates 45 g

EGGS

Eggs can definitely find their place in an anti-inflammatory diet, as they contain valuable nutrients such as high-quality proteins, B vitamins, selenium, and omega-3 fatty acids (especially in eggs from free-range hens). These ingredients can support the immune system and contribute to general health. However, some people are sensitive to eggs or specific components of eggs, which can lead to inflammatory reactions. Therefore, it is important to consider individual tolerance. It is generally advisable to look for organic quality eggs from free-range hens, as these can have a more favorable nutrient profile. In terms of quantity, a moderate consumption of around 3–4 eggs per week is a healthy addition to an anti-inflammatory diet for most people, provided there is no specific intolerance.

HEARTY BREAKFAST BOWL

Easy

Portions

25 Minutes

Vegan

Gluten-free

Nut-free

INGREDIENTS

5 oz	quinoa, thoroughly rinsed	1	avocado, diced
1 ¼ cups	vegetable stock (gluten-free)	1	handful of fresh spinach
2 tbsp	extra virgin olive oil	Juice of ½ lemon	
1	small red onion, finely diced	Salt and freshly ground black pepper to taste	
1 tsp	turmeric powder		
½ tsp	paprika powder	**Optional:** 1 tbsp chopped fresh herbs (e.g., parsley or coriander)	
7 oz	cherry tomatoes, halved		

PREPARATION

1. Place the quinoa and vegetable stock in a pan and bring to a boil. Reduce the heat, cover, and simmer for 15 minutes until the quinoa is soft, and the liquid has been completely absorbed.

2. Meanwhile, heat the olive oil in a frying pan over medium heat. Add the red onion and fry for 3–4 minutes until softened.

3. Stir in the turmeric and paprika powder and cook for 1 additional minute.

4. Add the halved cherry tomatoes and spinach, stir, and cook for 2–3 minutes until the spinach is wilted.

5. Add the finished quinoa to the pan, stir well, and remove from the heat. Season to taste with lemon juice, salt and pepper.

6. Divide the quinoa and vegetable mixture into bowls, garnish with diced avocado, and sprinkle with fresh herbs (optional).

Nutritional information (per portion)
Calories 350 kcal; Protein 9 g; Fat 15 g;
Sugar 3 g; Carbohydrates 45 g

SUPER GREEN FRITTATA BITES

 Medium   **Portions**   **35 Minutes** incl. preparation & baking time   **Vegetarian**   **Lactose-free**   **Nut-free**

INGREDIENTS

3.5 oz	broccoli, cut into small florets
6	egg yolks
7 oz	fresh spinach, roughly chopped
4	spring onions, finely chopped
2 tbsp	fresh parsley, chopped
¼ tsp	freshly ground black pepper
6	egg whites
Sea salt	

PREPARATION

1. Preheat the oven to 360 °F (180 °C). Lightly grease a mini muffin tray with 24 wells with cooking spray.

2. Place the broccoli in a small pan of boiling water and blanch for 2–3 minutes until just tender. Then rinse under cold water to stop the cooking process and preserve the bright-green color. Leave to cool completely.

3. Combine the egg yolks, spinach, spring onions, parsley, salt, pepper, and cooled broccoli in a large bowl and whisk them together.

4. Beat egg whites in a medium bowl with an electric mixer on high speed until stiff, about 2 minutes. Gently fold one-third of the beaten egg whites into the egg yolk mixture; repeat twice until all the beaten egg whites are folded in. Pour the egg mixture into the prepared muffin tray, filling each cavity completely.

5. Bake in the preheated oven until the center is set, about 8 minutes. Leave to cool in the tray for 2 minutes. Remove the bites from the tray and serve warm on a wire rack or allow to cool completely, about 20 minutes, and store in an airtight container in the refrigerator for up to 5 days.

NOTE

Carefully folding the beaten egg whites into the egg yolk mixture is crucial to achieve a soufflé-like texture. These Super Green Frittata Bites are protein-rich and contain anti-inflammatory ingredients such as broccoli, spinach, and parsley.

Nutritional information (per portion)
Calories 112 kcal; Protein 9 g; Fat 7 g; Sugar 1 g; Carbohydrates 2 g

MEAT

Conscious consumption of meat is essential in an anti-inflammatory diet. Preference should be given to lean meats such as poultry or lean beef, as they provide high-quality proteins without containing high amounts of inflammation-promoting saturated fatty acids. When eaten in moderation, these types of meat can contribute to muscle repair and maintenance without promoting negative inflammatory processes in the body. It is recommended to consume around 2–3 portions per week. Preparation is important: boiling, baking, or steaming are methods that can minimize the formation of harmful compounds, as opposed to roasting or grilling at high heat.

CHICKEN QUINOA BOWL

Medium	Portions	45 Minutes	Gluten-free	Lactose-free	Nut-free

INGREDIENTS

5 oz	quinoa, well rinsed
1 ¼ cups	vegetable stock
2	chicken breast fillets
1 tbsp	olive oil
1 tsp	turmeric powder
½ tsp	paprika powder
1	sweet potato, diced
1	red bell pepper, cut into strips
1	avocado, diced
1	handful of fresh spinach

Juice of 1/2 lemon

Salt and freshly ground black pepper

Optional: fresh herbs such as parsley or coriander to garnish

PREPARATION

1. Bring the quinoa to a boil in a pan with the vegetable stock, reduce the heat, and simmer, covered, for about 15 minutes until the liquid has been absorbed, and the quinoa is soft.

2. Marinate the chicken breast fillets with olive oil, turmeric powder, paprika powder, salt, and pepper. Fry in a pan over medium heat for 5–7 minutes on each side until cooked through. Then, cut into strips or dice.

3. Spread the sweet potato cubes on a baking tray lined with baking paper, drizzle with a little olive oil, and bake at 400 °F (200 °C) for about 20 minutes until soft.

4. Fry the red peppers in a pan for 2–3 minutes until they are slightly soft.

5. Arrange the cooked quinoa, roasted chicken, baked sweet potato cubes, roasted peppers, fresh spinach, and diced avocado in a bowl.

6. Drizzle with lemon juice and optionally garnish with fresh herbs.

Nutritional information (per portion)
Calories 500 kcal; Protein 30 g; Fat 15 g;
Sugar 5 g; Carbohydrates 65 g

CHICKEN WRAP

Easy

Portions

30 Minutes

Gluten-free

Lactose-free

Nut-free

INGREDIENTS

2	chicken breast fillets, cut into strips
2 tbsp	olive oil
1 tsp	turmeric powder
½ tsp	ground ginger
4	gluten-free wraps
1	avocado, cut into slices
1	small red bell pepper, cut into thin strips
1	carrot, thinly sliced or grated
1 tbsp	linseed
1	handful fresh spinach

Salt and freshly ground black pepper

Optional: A squeeze of lemon juice or a little tahini as a dressing

PREPARATION

1. Marinate chicken breast strips with 1 tbsp olive oil, turmeric powder, ground ginger, salt, and pepper. Heat the remaining olive oil in a frying pan over medium heat and fry the chicken strips for about 5–7 minutes until cooked through and lightly browned.

2. Prepare gluten-free wraps according to pack instructions, usually by gently heating them in a dry frying pan.

3. Spread the wraps out on a clean surface and top first with fresh spinach, then avocado, red bell pepper strips, and carrots.

4. Spread the fried chicken strips evenly over the wraps.

5. Optionally, add a squeeze of lemon juice or a little tahini over the filling for extra flavor.

6. Carefully roll up the wraps so that the filling is well enclosed.

7. Cut the wraps in half diagonally and serve.

CHICKEN

When using chicken, make sure it is organic or free-range. The chicken in this recipe is flavored with turmeric, a powerful anti-inflammatory spice that can reduce inflammation in the body through its active ingredient, curcumin.

Nutritional information (per serving)
Calories 400 kcal; Protein 25 g; Fat 20 g; Sugar 3 g; Carbohydrates 35 g

CHICKEN WRAP

WITH PEANUT-COCONUT SAUCE

 Easy   Portions (4)   30 Minutes   Lactose-free

INGREDIENTS

14 oz	chicken breast fillet, cut into strips	1 tbsp	coconut oil
4	wholemeal wraps	½ tsp	turmeric powder
		½ tsp	paprika powder
		Salt and freshly ground black pepper	

FOR THE SAUCE

2 tbsp	unsweetened peanut butter	1 tsp	fresh ginger, grated
1 tbsp	tamari (gluten-free soy sauce)	1	clove of garlic, finely chopped
¾ cup	coconut milk	½ tsp	turmeric powder
		Salt and freshly ground black pepper	

FOR THE FILLING

1	avocado, cut into slices	1	small red bell pepper, cut into strips
1	small carrot, julienne cut	Fresh coriander leaves	
1	handful of fresh spinach		

PREPARATION

1. Heat the coconut oil in a frying pan and season the chicken breast strips with turmeric powder, paprika powder, salt, and pepper. Fry over medium heat until golden brown on all sides and cooked through. Remove from the pan and set aside.

2. For the peanut coconut sauce, heat the peanut butter, tamari, coconut milk, grated ginger, chopped garlic, and turmeric powder in a small saucepan over low heat until smooth and well combined. Season to taste with salt and pepper if required.

3. Heat the gluten-free wraps according to the packet instructions.

4. Top each wrap with fresh spinach, avocado slices, julienne cut carrot, red bell pepper strips, and fried chicken strips.

5. Pour the warm peanut and coconut sauce over the filling and garnish with fresh coriander leaves.

6. Carefully roll up the wraps and serve immediately.

Nutritional information (per portion)
Calories 450 kcal; Protein 30 g; Fat 25 g;
Sugar 4 g; Carbohydrates 35 g

CURRY WITH RICE

 Easy   Portions   30 Minutes   Gluten free   Lactose-free   Nut-free

INGREDIENTS

7 oz	whole-grain basmati rice
1 ⅔ cups	coconut milk
1.1 lbs	lamb, cut into cubes
1 tbsp	coconut oil
1	onion, finely chopped
2	cloves of garlic, finely chopped
¾ inch	fresh ginger, peeled and finely chopped
1 tsp	turmeric powder
1 tsp	ground coriander
½ tsp	ground cumin
½ tsp	paprika powder
1	sweet potato, diced
1	bell pepper, cut into strips
7 oz	fresh spinach

Salt and freshly ground black pepper

Fresh coriander to garnish

Lemon wedges to serve

PREPARATION

1. Cook the whole-grain basmati rice according to package instructions.

2. Heat the coconut oil in a large saucepan or deep-frying pan over medium heat. Add the onion, garlic, and ginger and fry for 2–3 minutes until soft.

3. Add turmeric powder, ground coriander, cumin, and paprika powder, and stir well to activate the spices.

4. Add the lamb to the pot and fry for 10–15 minutes, stirring occasionally, until lightly browned all over.

5. Add the coconut milk, diced sweet potato, and bell pepper strips, stir well, and bring to a boil. Reduce the heat and simmer the curry for 30–45 minutes until the lamb is cooked through, and the vegetables are soft.

6. Add the fresh spinach and cook, stirring, for 2–3 minutes until it collapses.

7. Season to taste with salt and pepper. Serve the curry with cooked whole-grain basmati rice. Garnish with fresh coriander and lemon wedges.

Nutritional information (per portion)
Calories 550 kcal; Protein 30 g; Fat 20 g; Sugar 5 g; Carbohydrates 65 g

VEGETABLE AND MEAT STEW

 Easy Portions 30 Minutes Gluten-free Lactose-free Nut-free

INGREDIENTS

1 lb	beef, cut into cubes
2 tbsp	olive oil
2	carrots, diced
2	stalks of celery, finely chopped
1	onion, diced
2	cloves of garlic, finely chopped
14 oz	peeled tinned tomatoes, roughly chopped
2 cups	beef or vegetable stock
1 tsp	turmeric powder
1 tsp	paprika powder
½ tsp	ground ginger
1 bay	leaf
7 oz	sweet potatoes, diced
7 oz	zucchini, diced

Salt and freshly ground black pepper

Fresh herbs such as parsley or coriander to garnish

PREPARATION

1. In a large saucepan, heat the olive oil over medium heat. Add the beef cubes and brown on all sides until evenly browned. Remove from the pan and set aside.

2. In the same pot, add carrots, celery, onion and garlic. Sauté for 5–7 minutes, stirring occasionally, until the vegetables soften.

3. Return the browned beef to the pot. Add the peeled tomatoes, stock, turmeric powder, paprika powder, ground ginger, and bay leaf. Stir well.

4. Bring to a boil, then reduce the heat and simmer the covered stew over low heat for 1 hour until the meat is tender.

5. Add the sweet potatoes and zucchini and simmer for 20–30 minutes until all the vegetables are tender.

6. Season to taste with salt and pepper. Before serving, remove the bay leaf and garnish the stew with fresh herbs.

Nutritional information (per portion)
Calories 350 kcal; Protein 25 g; Fat 15 g
Sugar 5 g; Carbohydrates 30 g

CHICKEN SKEWERS

WITH VEGETABLES

 Easy
 Portions
 45 Minutes incl. marinating time
 Gluten-free
 Lactose-free
 Nut-free

INGREDIENTS

14 oz	chicken breast, cut into cubes
2 tbsp	olive oil
1 tsp	turmeric powder
1 tsp	ground coriander
½ tsp	paprika powder
1	zucchini, cut into slices
1	red bell pepper, cut into pieces
1	yellow bell pepper, cut into pieces
1	red onion, cut into wedges

Juice of 1 lemon

Salt and freshly ground black pepper

Wooden or metal skewers

PREPARATION

1. In a large bowl, mix olive oil, turmeric powder, ground coriander, paprika powder, lemon juice, salt, and pepper to create a marinade.

2. Add the chicken cubes to the marinade and stir well so that all the pieces are evenly coated. Leave to marinate in the fridge for at least 30 minutes.

3. Prepare the zucchini, red and yellow peppers, and red onion. Then, thread them onto the skewers, alternating with the marinated chicken cubes.

4. Preheat the grill or grill pan. Grill the skewers over medium heat on all sides until the chicken is cooked through, and the vegetables are soft but still firm to the bite, about 10–15 minutes.

5. Arrange the finished skewers on a plate and optionally drizzle with fresh lemon juice before serving.

Nutritional information (per portion)
Calories 350 kcal; Protein 25 g; Fat 15 g
Sugar 5 g; Carbohydrates 30 g

GLUTEN-FREE CHICKEN STRIPS

FROM THE OVEN

 Easy   Portions **4**   40 Minutes   Gluten-free   Lactose-free

INGREDIENTS

1 lb	chicken breast fillets, cut into strips
¼ cup	almond flour
¼ cup	coconut flour
1 tsp	paprika powder
½ tsp	garlic powder
½ tsp	onion powder
½ tsp	turmeric powder
2	large eggs
1 tbsp	extra virgin olive oil

Salt and freshly ground black pepper

PREPARATION

1. Preheat the oven to 400 °F (200 °C) and line a baking tray with baking paper. Brush the baking paper lightly with olive oil.

2. In a shallow bowl, mix the almond flour, coconut flour, paprika powder, garlic powder, onion powder, turmeric powder, black pepper, and sea salt.

3. Whisk the eggs in another bowl.

4. Dip the chicken strips first in the egg mixture so they are coated all over, and then turn them in the flour mixture until they are evenly coated.

5. Place the breaded chicken strips on the prepared baking tray and brush lightly with olive oil.

6. Bake in the preheated oven for about 25–30 minutes until the chicken strips are golden brown and cooked through. Turn once halfway through so that they brown evenly.

7. Remove the chicken strips from the oven and allow to cool briefly before serving.

Nutritional information (per serving)
Calories 300 kcal; Protein 35 g; Fat 15 g;
Sugar 1 g; Carbohydrates 10 g

AVOCADO CHICKEN SALAD

 Easy   Portions   30 Minutes   Gluten-free   Lactose-free   Nut-free

INGREDIENTS

2	chicken breast fillets, cooked and cut into pieces
2	ripe avocados, diced
½	red onion, finely chopped
2 tbsp	extra virgin olive oil
1 tsp	apple cider vinegar
½ tsp	turmeric powder
1	handful of cherry tomatoes, halved
1	handful of fresh spinach
1	handful of rocket

Juice of 1 lemon

Salt and freshly ground black pepper

Optional: chopped fresh herbs such as parsley or coriander

PREPARATION

1. In a large bowl, mix lemon juice, olive oil, apple cider vinegar, turmeric powder, salt, and pepper to create the dressing.

2. Add the cooked and chopped chicken breast fillets, diced avocados, finely chopped red onion, and halved cherry tomatoes to the dressing.

3. Add the fresh spinach and rocket and mix gently, so the avocado does not turn to mush.

4. Optionally garnish with fresh herbs such as parsley or coriander.

5. Arrange the salad on plates and serve immediately.

Nutritional information (per portion)
Calories 400 kcal; Protein 25 g; Fat 30 g;
Sugar 3 g; Carbohydrates 15 g

ORIENTAL MEATLOAF

WITH CHICKPEAS AND EGGPLANT

 Medium   Portions   1 Hour 20 Minutes   Gluten-free   Lactose-free   Nut-free

CHICKPEAS

Chickpeas are a key element in the anti-inflammatory diet thanks to their high fiber, protein, and antioxidant content. They promote gut health, stabilize blood sugar levels, and provide protection against oxidative stress, which helps to reduce inflammation in the body. Due to their nutrient-rich composition, chickpeas effectively support the fight against chronic inflammation and strengthen overall health.

INGREDIENTS

1 lb	veal, finely chopped
1	large eggplant, cut into small cubes
1 tin	of chickpeas, rinsed and drained
2 tbsp	extra virgin olive oil
1	large onion, finely diced
2	cloves of garlic, finely chopped
1 tsp	turmeric powder
1 tsp	paprika powder
½ tsp	ground cumin
½ tsp	ground coriander
2 tbsp	tomato paste

Salt and freshly ground black pepper

A little less than ½ cup vegetable stock (gluten-free)

Fresh herbs (e.g., parsley) to garnish

PREPARATION

1. Preheat the oven to 360 °F (180 °C).

2. Fry the eggplant cubes in a pan with 1 tbsp olive oil over medium heat for 5–7 minutes until soft. Remove from the pan and set aside.

3. Heat the remaining tablespoon of olive oil in the same pan. Add the onion and garlic and fry for 2–3 minutes until soft.

4. Add the turmeric powder, paprika powder, cumin, and coriander and cook for 1 minute with the onions and garlic.

5. Add the veal to the pan. Add the tomato purée and stir well. Cook the mixture for 5 minutes until the meat is browned.

6. Add the chickpeas, pre-fried diced eggplant, and vegetable stock. Season with salt and pepper and mix well.

7. Place the mince mixture in a greased baking dish and smooth out.

8. Bake in the preheated oven for about 40–45 minutes until the meatloaf is firm and golden brown.

9. Remove the meatloaf from the oven before serving, allow it to cool briefly, and garnish it with fresh herbs.

Nutritional information (per portion)
Calories 350 kcal; Protein 25 g; Fat 20 g;
Sugar 5 g; Carbohydrates 15 g

CHICKEN SOUP

Easy

Portions

1 Hour

Gluten-free

Lactose-free

Nut-free

INGREDIENTS

1 lb	chicken breast, cut into small pieces
2 tbsp	olive oil
1	large onion, finely diced
2	carrots, diced
2	stalks of celery, sliced
2	cloves of garlic, finely chopped
1 tsp	turmeric powder
1 tsp	ginger powder

1	bay leaf
½ tsp	dried thyme

About 4 ¼ cups chicken stock (gluten-free)

Juice of ½ lemon

Salt and freshly ground black pepper

Fresh parsley to garnish

Optional: ½ tsp cayenne pepper (optional; adjust according to spiciness preference)

PREPARATION

1. In a large saucepan, heat the olive oil over medium heat. Add the onion, carrots, celery, and garlic, and sauté for 5–7 minutes until the vegetables soften.

2. Add the chicken breast pieces and sauté for about 5 minutes until white on all sides.

3. Add the chicken stock, turmeric powder, ginger powder, cayenne pepper, bay leaf, and thyme to the pan. Season with salt and pepper and bring to a boil.

4. Reduce the heat and simmer the soup, covered, over low heat for 30–40 minutes until the chicken is fully cooked through.

5. Remove the bay leaf and squeeze the juice of half a lemon into the soup. Stir well.

6. Pour the soup into bowls and garnish with freshly chopped parsley.

7. Serve hot.

Nutritional information (per porttion)
Calories 250 kcal; Protein 20 g; Fat 10 g;
Sugar 3 g; Carbohydrates 15 g

PEPPER

Pepper, especially black pepper, is a powerful spice in the anti-inflammatory diet. It contains piperine, a compound that stimulates the digestive tract and significantly increases curcumin's bioavailability - the active anti-inflammatory component in turmeric. This synergy enhances the anti-inflammatory effects of both spices, helping to relieve inflammatory symptoms and promote overall health. In addition, pepper has antioxidant properties that fight free radicals and thus protect the body from oxidative stress. A pinch of black pepper in meals can enhance the anti-inflammatory effect of food and positively impact health.

FISH

SALMON

Salmon is known for its anti-inflammatory benefits from omega-3 fatty acids, which improve heart health and reduce the risk of chronic diseases. It is also rich in vitamin D and selenium, which strengthens the immune system. Eating two portions of salmon a week can reduce inflammation and support overall health.

SALMON WITH CRUST

AND VEGETABLES

Medium Portions 40 Minutes Gluten-free Lactose-free Nut-free

INGREDIENTS

4	salmon fillets (approx. 5 oz each, with skin)	2 tbsp	extra virgin olive oil

FOR THE CRUST

½ cup	flaked almonds	1	clove of garlic, finely chopped
2 tbsp	fresh parsley, finely chopped		Zest of 1 lemon
1 tbsp	fresh dill, finely chopped		Salt and freshly ground black pepper

FOR THE VEGETABLES

7 oz	green asparagus, ends cut off	1	zucchini, cut into slices
1	red bell pepper, cut into strips	2 tbsp	extra virgin olive oil
1	yellow bell pepper, cut into strips		Salt and freshly ground black pepper

PREPARATION

1. Preheat the oven to 400 °F (200 °C).

2. For the crust, mix the flaked almonds, chopped parsley, dill, lemon zest, chopped garlic, salt and pepper in a small bowl.

3. Place the salmon fillets on a baking tray lined with baking paper. Drizzle each fillet with 1/2 tbsp olive oil and spread the crust mixture evenly over the salmon fillets, pressing down lightly.

4. Mix the chopped vegetables in another bowl with 2 tbsp olive oil, salt, and pepper until everything is well coated.

5. Spread the vegetables around the salmon fillets on the baking tray.

6. Place the baking tray in the preheated oven and bake for 20–25 minutes until the salmon is cooked, and the crust is golden brown.

7. Arrange the salmon fillets on plates with the vegetables before serving.

Nutritional information (per portion)
Calories 400 kcal; Protein 25 g; Fat 28 g;
Sugar 4 g; Carbohydrates 10 g

SALMON AND AVOCADO SALAD

 Easy
 Portions
 30 Minutes
 Gluten-free
 Lactose-free
 Nut-free

INGREDIENTS

2	salmon fillets (approx. 5 oz each, with skin)	1	small cucumber, cut into slices
2 tbsp	olive oil	½	red onion, cut into thin rings
1	ripe avocado, diced	10	cherry tomatoes, halved
1	handful of mixed leaf lettuce (e.g., spinach, rocket, lamb's lettuce)		

FOR THE DRESSING

3 tbsp	extra virgin olive oil	1	clove of garlic, finely chopped
1 tbsp	apple cider vinegar		Juice of ½ lemon
1 tsp	mustard		Salt and freshly ground black pepper
1 tsp	honey (optional)		

PREPARATION

1. Preheat the oven to 400 °F (200 °C). Brush the salmon fillets with 1 tbsp olive oil, season with salt and pepper, and place on a baking tray lined with baking paper. Bake in the oven for about 15–20 minutes until the salmon is cooked through.

2. Meanwhile, for the dressing, whisk together the olive oil, apple cider vinegar, lemon juice, mustard, honey (if using), chopped garlic, salt and pepper in a small bowl until well combined.

3. In a large salad bowl, combine the mixed lettuce leaves, cucumber slices, red onion rings, cherry tomatoes, and diced avocado.

4. Carefully cut the baked salmon fillet into smaller pieces and place on top of the salad.

5. Pour the dressing over the salad and mix everything together carefully.

Nutritional information (per portion)
Calories 450 kcal; Protein 25 g; Fat 35 g; Sugar 4 g; Carbohydrates 12 g

GRILLED SHRIMP SALAD

Easy

Portions

30 Minutes

Gluten-free

Lactose-free

Nut-free

INGREDIENTS

1 lb	shrimp, peeled and deveined	½	red onion, cut into thin rings
2 tbsp	olive oil	½	cucumber, sliced
1 tsp	paprika powder	10	cherry tomatoes, halved
½ tsp	turmeric powder	1	handful of mixed leaf lettuce (e.g., spinach, rocket)
½ tsp	ground ginger		
1	avocado, diced		Salt and freshly ground black pepper

FOR THE SAUCE

3 tbsp	extra virgin olive oil	1 tsp	Dijon mustard
1 tbsp	lemon juice	1 tsp	honey (optional)
1 tbsp	apple cider vinegar		Salt and freshly ground black pepper

PREPARATION

1. Marinate the shrimp with 1 tbsp olive oil, paprika powder, turmeric powder, ground ginger, salt, and pepper. Leave to stand in the fridge for at least 10 minutes.

2. Heat a grill pan over medium heat and grill the marinated shrimp on each side for 2–3 minutes until they are pink and lightly browned. Set aside and leave to cool.

3. For the dressing, whisk together the olive oil, lemon juice, apple cider vinegar, Dijon mustard, honey (if using), salt and pepper in a small bowl.

4. In a large salad bowl, mix together the lettuce leaves, avocado cubes, red onion rings, cucumber slices, and cherry tomatoes.

5. Spread the grilled shrimp over the salad

6. Pour the dressing over the salad and stir gently to mix all the ingredients.

Nutritional information (per portion)
Calories 350 kcal; Protein 25 g; Fat 22 g;
Sugar 3 g; Carbohydrates 10 g

HERRING

WITH POTATO GRATIN

 Medium   **Portions** 4   **1 Hour 15 Minutes**   **Gluten-free**   **Lactose-free**

INGREDIENTS

4 — fresh herring fillets

2 tbsp — olive oil

FOR THE POTATO GRATIN

1.8 lbs — potatoes, peeled and cut into thin slices

1 ⅔ cups — coconut milk

2 — cloves of garlic, finely chopped

1 tsp — turmeric powder

½ tsp — nutmeg, freshly grated

Salt and freshly ground black pepper

TO GARNISH

Fresh dill sprigs

PREPARATION

1. Preheat the oven to 360 °F (180 °C).

2. For the potato gratin, mix the coconut milk, chopped garlic, turmeric powder, nutmeg, salt, and pepper in a large bowl.

3. Add the potato slices and toss in the mixture until they are evenly coated

4. Layer the potatoes in a greased baking dish and pour the remaining coconut milk mixture over them.

5. Bake the potato gratin in the preheated oven for about 45–50 minutes until the potatoes are tender and a golden-brown crust has formed.

6. While the gratin is baking, rinse the herring fillets under cold water and pat dry. Season with salt and pepper.

7. Heat the olive oil in a frying pan and fry the herring fillets on each side for 2–3 minutes until they are cooked through and slightly golden.

8. Arrange the fried herring fillets on a plate, add the finished potato gratin, and garnish with fresh dill.

9. Serve immediately.

Nutritional information (per portion)
Calories 550 kcal; Protein 25 g; Fat 30 g; Sugar 5 g; Carbohydrates 45 g

TURMERIC

Turmeric is a key element in the anti-inflammatory diet, primarily because of its active ingredient, curcumin, which is known for its powerful anti-inflammatory and antioxidant properties. Curcumin can help reduce inflammatory processes in the body associated with various chronic diseases and support overall health. Regularly including turmeric in the diet, often combined with black pepper to improve absorption, can thus reduce the risk of inflammatory diseases and promote well-being.

FRIED PRAWNS

WITH VEGETABLES AND QUINOA

 Easy Portions 40 Minutes Gluten-free Lactose-free Nut-free

INGREDIENTS

1 lb	prawns, peeled and deveined
2 tbsp	olive oil
1 tsp	turmeric powder
½ tsp	paprika powder
¼ tsp	ground ginger
1	red bell pepper, cut into strips
1	zucchini, cut into half-moons
1	small red onion, cut into wedges
1	handful of cherry tomatoes, halved
7 oz	quinoa
1 ⅔	cups vegetable stock (gluten-free)

Salt and freshly ground black pepper

Fresh coriander or parsley to garnish

PREPARATION

1. Rinse the quinoa in a sieve under running water to remove any bitterness. Bring the vegetable stock to a boil in a pan, add the quinoa, reduce the heat, cover, and simmer for 15–20 minutes until the liquid has been absorbed. Remove from the heat and leave to soak.

2. Heat 1 tbsp olive oil in a large frying pan over medium heat. Season the prawns with turmeric powder, paprika powder, ground ginger, salt, and pepper, and add to the pan. Fry on each side for 2–3 minutes until pink and cooked through. Remove from the pan and set aside.

3. Heat the remaining tablespoon of olive oil in the same pan. Add the red bell pepper, zucchini, and red onion and fry for 5–7 minutes, stirring occasionally, until the vegetables are soft. Add the cherry tomatoes and cook for another 2 minutes.

4. Return the fried prawns to the pan, mix well, and season with salt and pepper if necessary.

5. Serve the fried prawns and vegetables with the quinoa side dish. Garnish with fresh coriander or parsley.

Nutritional information (per portion)
Calories 450 kcal; Protein 30 g; Fat 18 g;
Sugar 6 g; Carbohydrates 45 g

GREEN CURRY

WITH HALIBUT AND BROWN RICE

 Medium   **Portions**   **45 Minutes**   **Gluten-free**   **Lactose-free**   **Nut-free**

INGREDIENTS

0.9 lbs	halibut fillet, cut into large pieces
2 tbsp	olive oil
1	onion, finely diced
2	cloves of garlic, finely chopped
1	piece of fresh ginger (¾ inches), finely chopped
2 tbsp	green curry paste
1 ⅔ cups	coconut milk

1	red bell pepper, cut into strips
1	small zucchini, cut into half-moons
3.5 oz	green beans, cleaned and halved

A little less than 1 cup vegetable stock (gluten-free)

Juice of 1 lime

Salt and freshly ground black pepper

Fresh coriander to garnish

FOR THE SIDE DISH

7 oz	brown rice

PREPARATION

1. Cook the brown rice according to the packet instructions. Set aside and keep warm.

2. In a large saucepan or deep-frying pan, heat the olive oil over medium heat. Add the onion, garlic, ginger, and sauté for 2–3 minutes until soft.

3. Add the green curry paste and cook for 1 minute, stirring to release the flavors.

4. Stir in the coconut milk and vegetable stock and bring to a boil.

5. Add the red bell pepper, zucchini, and green beans to the curry and simmer for 10 minutes until the vegetables are soft but still firm enough to bite.

6. Add the halibut pieces and simmer over low heat for 5–7 minutes until the fish is cooked through.

7. Season to taste with lime juice, salt, and pepper.

8. Arrange the green curry with halibut on plates, pour over the cooked brown rice, and garnish with fresh coriander.

Nutritional information (per portion)
Calories 600 kcal; Protein 30 g; Fat 35 g; Sugar 5 g; Carbohydrates 45 g

GINGER

———

Ginger is a powerful spice in the anti-inflammatory diet, prized for its pain-relieving and anti-inflammatory properties. The gingerols contained in ginger have an antioxidant effect and can help suppress inflammatory processes in the body. This makes ginger particularly useful in relieving joint pain, digestive discomfort, and other inflammation-related conditions.

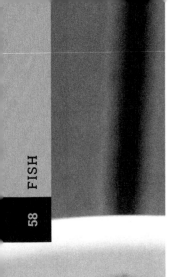

THAI SALMON
WITH QUINOA

Easy   Portions   40 Minutes   Gluten-free   Lactose-free   Nut-free

INGREDIENTS

4	salmon fillets (approx. 5 oz each)	7 oz	quinoa
		2 tbsp	extra virgin olive oil

FOR THE SAUCE

3 tbsp	tamari (gluten-free soy sauce)	1 tsp	fresh ginger, grated
2 tbsp	lime juice	1	clove of garlic, finely chopped
1 tbsp	maple syrup	½ tsp	turmeric powder

TO GARNISH

1	red chili, deseeded

Finely chopped Fresh coriander leaves

TO SERVE

1	avocado, cut into slices	1	carrot, julienne cut
1	small cucumber, sliced		Lime wedges

PREPARATION

1. Cook the quinoa according to the packet instructions. Set aside and keep warm.

2. In a small bowl, whisk together the tamari, lime juice, maple syrup, grated ginger, chopped garlic, and turmeric powder to make the sauce.

3. Pat the salmon fillets dry and season with salt and pepper. Heat 1 tbsp olive oil in a large frying pan over medium heat. Sear the salmon fillets on the skin side for 5 minutes, turn them over, and cook an additional 3–4 minutes until cooked through.

4. Pour half of the prepared sauce over the salmon and allow to caramelize briefly.

5. Divide the cooked quinoa into bowls. Arrange the cooked salmon on top and drizzle with the remaining sauce.

6. Arrange the avocado, cucumber, and carrot salad and drape around the salmon. Garnish with fresh coriander, optional red chili, and lime wedges.

Nutritional information (per portion)
Calories 500 kcal; Protein 30 g; Fat 22 g;
Sugar 5 g; Carbohydrates 45 g

OVEN-BAKED FISH

Easy

Portions

35 Minutes

Gluten-free

Lactose-free

Nut-free

INGREDIENTS

1 lb	fish fillets (e.g., salmon or cod, approx. 5 oz each)
2 tbsp	olive oil
2	cloves of garlic, finely chopped
1 tsp	turmeric powder
1 tsp	paprika powder
½ tsp	ground ginger
2	sweet potatoes, diced
1	bunch green asparagus, ends cut off
1	red bell pepper, cut into strips

Salt and freshly ground black pepper

PREPARATION

1. Preheat the oven to 400 °F (200 °C). Line a large baking tray with baking paper.

2. In a small bowl, mix together the olive oil, chopped garlic, lemon juice and zest, turmeric powder, paprika powder, ground ginger, salt, and pepper to create a marinade.

3. Place the fish fillets in the marinade and make sure they are completely covered. Set aside and leave to marinate for at least 10 minutes.

4. Spread the sweet potatoes, green asparagus, and red bell pepper on the baking tray. Drizzle with half of the remaining marinade and season lightly with salt.

5. Place the marinated fish fillets on top of the vegetables and drizzle with the remaining marinade.

6. Bake in the preheated oven for about 20–25 minutes, or until the fish is cooked through, and the vegetables are tender.

7. Garnish with fresh herbs such as dill or parsley before serving.

Nutritional information (per portion)
Calories 350 kcal; Protein 25 g; Fat 15 g;
Sugar 5 g; Carbohydrates 25 g

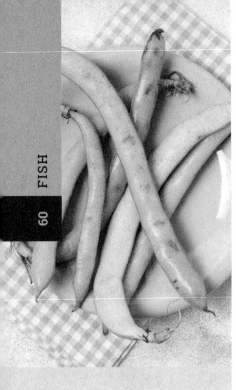

HONEY

Honey, especially in its raw and unfiltered form, can be a valuable addition to an anti-inflammatory diet. It contains antioxidants that fight inflammation and strengthen the immune system. Honey also has antibacterial properties that can contribute to digestive health. Its natural sweetness makes it a good substitute for industrial sugar, which can promote inflammatory processes. However, due to its sugar content, honey should be consumed in moderation to reap the benefits without adverse effects on blood sugar levels.

HONEY SOY SALMON

WITH SWEET POTATOES AND GREEN BEANS

| Easy | Portions | 40 Minutes | Gluten-free | Lactose-free | Nut-free |

INGREDIENTS

4	salmon fillets (approx. 5 oz each)	1 lb	green beans, ends cut off
2	large sweet potatoes, peeled and cut into cubes	2 tbsp	extra virgin olive oil

FOR THE MARINATED/SAUCE

3 tbsp	gluten-free soy sauce	1 tsp	turmeric powder
2 tbsp	honey		Salt and freshly ground black pepper
1 tbsp	fresh ginger, finely grated		Juice of ½ lemon
2	cloves of garlic, finely chopped		

PREPARATION

1. Preheat the oven to 400 °F (200 °C). Line a large baking tray with baking paper.

2. In a small bowl, whisk together the soy sauce, honey, grated ginger, chopped garlic, lemon juice, and turmeric powder to make the marinade/sauce. Season to taste with salt and pepper.

3. Mix the sweet potato cubes and green beans in a large bowl with 1 tbsp olive oil and half of the marinade/sauce until everything is evenly coated. Spread on the baking tray and bake in the oven for about 15 minutes.

4. Brush the salmon fillets with the remaining olive oil and place on top of the vegetables. Pour the remaining marinade/sauce evenly over the salmon.

5. Bake everything together for an additional 12–15 minutes, or until the salmon is cooked through, and the vegetables are tender.

6. Plate the honey soy salmon with sweet potatoes and green beans before serving.

Nutritional information (per portion)
Calories 450 kcal; Protein 25 g; Fat 20 g;
Sugar 12 g; Carbohydrates 40 g

FISH SOUP

 Medium
 Portions (4)
 40 Minutes
 Gluten-free
 Lactose-free
 Nut-free

INGREDIENTS

1 lb	fresh white fish (e.g., white fish, pollack), cut into bite-sized pieces
2 tbsp	olive oil
1	large onion, finely diced
2	cloves of garlic, finely chopped
1	piece of fresh ginger, finely grated
1 tsp	turmeric powder
½ tsp	paprika powder
¼ tsp	cayenne pepper
1 lb	can of peeled tomatoes, roughly chopped
1 liter	fish or vegetable stock (gluten-free)

Juice of 1 lemon

1 handful of fresh coriander, roughly chopped

Salt and freshly ground black pepper

PREPARATION

1. In a large saucepan, heat the olive oil over medium heat. Add the onion, garlic, and ginger and fry for 3–4 minutes, stirring, until the onion is soft.

2. Add the turmeric powder, paprika powder, and cayenne pepper and cook for another 1 minute, stirring to release the flavors.

3. Add the roughly chopped tomatoes and stock. Bring to a boil, then reduce the heat and simmer for 20 minutes.

4. Add the fish pieces to the soup and simmer over low heat for 10–12 minutes until the fish is cooked through and flakes easily with a fork.

5. Season to taste with lemon juice, salt and pepper. Stir in the fresh coriander before serving.

6. Pour the soup into bowls and serve hot.

Nutritional information (per portion)
Calories 250 kcal; Protein 25 g; Fat 10 g;
Sugar 4 g; Carbohydrates 10 g

VEGETARIAN
VEGAN

ANTI-INFLAMMATORY BOWL

Easy

2 Portions

45 Minutes

Vegan

Gluten-free

Nut-free

INGREDIENTS

5 oz	quinoa, well rinsed	1	handful of baby spinach
1 ¼ cups	vegetable stock	1	avocado, sliced
1	sweet potato, diced	½	cucumber, sliced
1 tbsp	extra virgin olive oil	3.5 oz	chickpeas
½ tsp	turmeric powder	1 tbsp	linseed
1	medium-sized beet, diced		

FOR THE DRESSING

2 tbsp	olive oil	1 tsp	maple syrup
1 tbsp	apple cider vinegar	Salt and freshly ground black pepper	
1 tsp	Dijon mustard		

PREPARATION

1. Bring the quinoa to a boil in a pan with the vegetable stock. Reduce the heat, cover, and simmer for about 15 minutes until the liquid has been absorbed, and the quinoa is soft.

2. Mix the sweet potato and beet cubes with olive oil and turmeric powder, place on a baking tray, and bake at 400 °F (200 °C) for about 20–25 minutes until soft and slightly caramelized.

3. For the dressing, whisk together the olive oil, apple cider vinegar, Dijon mustard, maple syrup, salt, and pepper in a small bowl.

4. Place the cooked quinoa in a bowl as a base. Top with baked sweet potato and beet, baby spinach, avocado slices, cucumber slices, and chickpeas.

5. Drizzle the anti-inflammatory bowl with the prepared dressing and sprinkle with linseed.

6. Mix everything lightly before serving, or enjoy as is.

Nutritional information (per portion)
Calories 500 kcal; Protein 15 g; Fat 25 g;
Sugar 8 g; Carbohydrates 60 g

STUFFED SWEET POTATOES

WITH SPINACH AND QUINOA

 Medium   **Portions** (4)   **1 Hour**   **Vegan**   **Gluten-free**   **Nut-free**

INGREDIENTS

4	medium sweet potatoes	7 oz	fresh spinach, roughly chopped
1	cup quinoa, well rinsed	1 tsp	turmeric powder
2	cups vegetable stock (gluten-free)	½ tsp	ground cumin
2 tbsp	olive oil		Salt and freshly ground black pepper
1	onion, finely diced		Juice of 1 lemon
2	cloves of garlic, finely chopped		Fresh herbs, such as parsley or coriander, to garnish

PREPARATION

1. Preheat the oven to 400 °F (200 °C). Wash the sweet potatoes thoroughly, dry them, and prick them several times with a fork. Place on a baking tray lined with baking paper and bake in the preheated oven for about 45–50 minutes until soft.

2. Meanwhile, bring the quinoa to a boil in a pan with the vegetable stock. Cover and simmer for about 15 minutes, reducing the heat, until the liquid is absorbed. Remove from the heat, cover, and leave to soak for an additional 5 minutes.

3. Heat the olive oil in a large frying pan over medium heat. Add the onion, garlic, and sauté for 2–3 minutes until the onion is soft.

4. Add the spinach, turmeric powder, and cumin. Cook, stirring, until the spinach collapses. Season with salt and pepper.

5. Fold the quinoa into the spinach mixture and mix well. Remove from the heat and season with lemon juice.

6. Slice the baked sweet potatoes length ways and carefully open them. Stuff the quinoa and spinach mixture evenly into the sweet potatoes.

7. Garnish with fresh herbs and serve.

Nutritional information (per portion)
Calories 300 kcal; Protein 8 g; Fat 7 g;
Sugar 5 g; Carbohydrates 50 g

SWEET POTATOES

———

Sweet potatoes are an excellent food for anti-inflammatory nutrition, rich in beta-carotene, vitamins (especially vitamins C and E), and minerals that act as powerful antioxidants and can reduce inflammation in the body. Their high fiber content also supports gut health and promotes a healthy microbiome.

CARROT TAGLIATELLE

WITH TOMATOES AND ROCKET

| Easy | Portions | 30 Minutes | Vegan | Gluten-free | Nut-free |

INGREDIENTS

4	large carrots, peeled and cut into tagliatelle shapes using a spiral cutter
2 tbsp	olive oil
2	cloves of garlic, finely chopped
7 oz	cherry tomatoes, halved
1	handful of rocket

Juice of 1 lemon

Salt and freshly ground black pepper

Optional: a few basil leaves to garnish

PREPARATION

1. In a large frying pan, heat the olive oil over medium heat. Add the garlic and fry for 1–2 minutes until fragrant but not browned.

2. Add the carrot tagliatelle and fry for about 5–7 minutes until soft but still somewhat crunchy.

3. Add the halved cherry tomatoes to the pan and cook for an additional 2–3 minutes until the tomatoes have softened slightly.

4. Fold in the rocket and season with lemon juice, salt and pepper. Mix everything well until the rocket has wilted slightly.

5. Arrange the carrot tagliatelle on plates and optionally garnish with fresh basil leaves.

Nutritional information (per portion)
Calories 150 kcal; Protein 2 g; Fat 10 g;
Sugar 8 g; Carbohydrates 14 g

DAL

WITH TURMERIC AND COCONUT

 Easy   Portions   45 Minutes   Vegan   Gluten-free   Nut-free

INGREDIENTS

1 cup	red lentils, well rinsed
1 tbsp	coconut oil
1	large onion, finely diced
2	cloves of garlic, finely chopped
1	piece of fresh ginger, finely grated
1 tsp	turmeric powder
1 tsp	ground coriander
½ tsp	ground cumin
¼ tsp	cayenne pepper (optional; adjust according to spiciness preference)
1 ⅔ cups	coconut milk
2 cups	vegetable stock (gluten-free)
	Juice of 1 lime
	Salt and freshly ground black pepper

TO SERVE

Fresh coriander, chopped   coconut chips

PREPARATION

1. In a large pot, heat coconut oil over medium heat. Add the onion, garlic, and ginger and fry for 3–4 minutes until the onion is soft and translucent.

2. Add the turmeric powder, ground coriander, cumin, and cayenne pepper. Stir well and cook for 1 minute to release the flavors.

3. Add the red lentils, coconut milk, and vegetable stock to the pan. Bring to a boil, then reduce the heat and simmer for 25–30 minutes until the lentils are soft, and the dal has reached a creamy consistency.

4. Season to taste with lime juice, salt, and pepper.

5. Pour the dal into bowls, garnish with fresh coriander and coconut chips, and serve.

Nutritional information (per portion)
Calories 350 kcal; Protein 12 g; Fat 18 g; Sugar 3 g; Carbohydrates 35 g

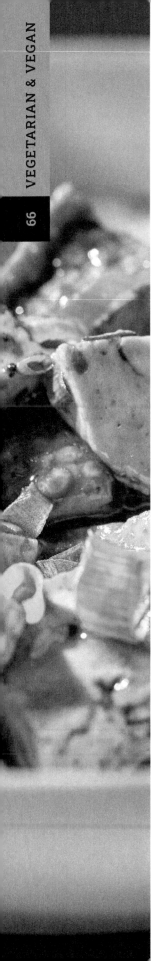

MARINATED TOFU

WITH VEGETABLES AND BROWN RICE

Medium

Portions

1 Hour
incl. marintatin time

Vegan

Gluten-free

Nut-free

INGREDIENTS

14 oz	firm tofu, drained and cut into cubes	**7 oz**	brown rice

FOR THE MARINADE

3 tbsp	tamari (gluten-free soy sauce)	**1 tsp**	ground ginger
2 tbsp	extra virgin olive oil	**1**	clove of garlic, finely chopped
1 tbsp	maple syrup		Juice of 1 lime
1 tsp	turmeric powder		

FOR THE VEGETABLES

1	medium sweet potato, diced	**1**	zucchini, cut into half-moons
1	red bell pepper, cut into strips	**2 tbsp**	extra virgin olive oil
		1	handful of green beans, ends cut off

Salt and freshly ground black pepper

PREPARATION

1. Marinate the tofu in a mixture of tamari, olive oil, maple syrup, turmeric powder, ground ginger, chopped garlic, and lime juice. Leave to marinate in the fridge for at least 30 minutes, or longer for a more intense flavor.

2. Cook the brown rice according to the packet instructions. Set aside and keep warm.

3. Preheat the oven to 400 °F (200 °C). Spread the diced sweet potato, red bell pepper, zucchini, and green beans on a baking tray lined with baking paper. Drizzle with olive oil, and season with salt and pepper. Roast in the oven for about 20–25 minutes until the vegetables are soft and slightly caramelized.

4. While the vegetables are in the oven, heat a frying pan over medium heat and remove the marinated tofu from the marinade (reserve the marinade). Fry the tofu on all sides until golden brown, about 5–7 minutes. Pour the remaining marinade over the tofu and bring to a boil briefly until thickened.

5. Divide the cooked brown rice between plates, arrange the roasted vegetables and marinated tofu on top.

6. Garnish with fresh herbs and serve immediately.

Nutritional information (per portion)
Calories 450 kcal; Protein 20 g; Fat 20 g;
Sugar 8 g; Carbohydrates 50 g

THAI ZOODLE BOWL

 Easy   **Portions**   **45 Minutes**   **Vegan**   **Gluten-free**   **Nut-free**

INGREDIENTS

14 oz	firm tofu, drained and cut into cubes
4	medium-sized zucchini, cut into spiral noodles (zoodles)
1	carrot, cut into noodles in a spiral shape
1	red bell pepper, cut into thin strips
¼ cup	unsalted peanuts, roughly chopped
1	handful green beans, halved

Fresh coriander to garnish

FOR THE MARINADE AND PEANUT SAUCE

3 tbsp	tamari (gluten-free soy sauce)
2 tbsp	maple syrup
1 tbsp	grated ginger
2	cloves of garlic, finely chopped
2 tbsp	lime juice
3 tbsp	natural peanut butter
¼ tsp	cayenne pepper (optional; adjust according to spiciness preference)

Water, to thin as required

PREPARATION

1. Marinate the tofu in a mixture of tamari, maple syrup, ginger, garlic, and half of the lime juice. Allow to stand in the fridge for at least 30 minutes.

2. For the peanut sauce, mix the peanut butter with the remaining tamari, maple syrup, ginger, garlic, lime juice, and cayenne pepper in a bowl. Add water as needed until the desired consistency is reached.

3. Heat a frying pan over medium heat and fry the marinated tofu on all sides until golden brown without any additional oil. Set aside.

4. In the same pan, sauté the zoodles, carrot noodles, red bell pepper, and green beans with a splash of water for about 3–5 minutes until the vegetables are slightly soft but still have a bite.

5. Divide the vegetables between bowls, place the fried tofu on top, and pour the peanut sauce over it.

TOFU

Tofu is an excellent food for an anti-inflammatory diet, thanks to its isoflavones, which have antioxidant and anti-inflammatory effects. As a plant-based source of protein, tofu supports health and can reduce the risk of chronic diseases. Versatile, tofu is ideal for a nutrient-rich, plant-based diet.

Nutritional information (per serving)
Calories 400 kcal; Protein 20 g; Fat 25 g; Sugar 10 g; Carbohydrates 25 g

VEGAN OR VEGETARIAN

A vegetarian or vegan diet can be effectively anti-inflammatory because it is rich in plant based foods that contain abundant antioxidants, phytonutrients, and fiber. These nutrients help to reduce oxidative damage and inflammation in the body. Plant-based diets emphasize the consumption of fruits, vegetables, whole grains, legumes, nuts, and seeds, all of which have natural anti-inflammatory properties. They also avoid or reduce the consumption of processed meats and animal fats, which can promote inflammation. Increasing the proportion of plant-based foods, such as a vegan or vegetarian diet, can help prevent and control inflammatory processes and promote general health.

ROASTED VEGETABLES

ON POLENTA

| Medium | Portions | 1 Hour | Vegan | Gluten-free | Nut-free |

INGREDIENTS

FOR THE POLENTA

1 cup	polenta (corn semolina)	2 tbsp	extra virgin olive oil
4 cups	vegetable stock (gluten-free)	Salt to taste	

FOR THE ROASTED VEGETABLES

2	medium zucchini, sliced	1 tsp	turmeric powder
2	red peppers, cut into strips	½ tsp	ground ginger
1	eggplant, cut into slices	½ tsp	paprika powder
7 oz	cherry tomatoes, halved	Salt and freshly ground black pepper	
2 tbsp	extra virgin olive oil	Fresh herbs, such as parsley or basil, to garnish	

PREPARATION

1. Bring the vegetable stock to a boil in a large pan. Slowly pour in the polenta while stirring. Reduce the heat and simmer for 30–40 minutes, stirring frequently, until the polenta is thick and creamy. Finally, stir in the olive oil and season with salt. Keep warm.

2. Mix the vegetables with the olive oil, turmeric powder, ground ginger, paprika, salt, and pepper in a large bowl until everything is evenly coated.

3. Heat a large frying pan over medium heat. Add the marinated vegetables in batches and fry on all sides until soft and lightly browned. Fry in batches if necessary to avoid overcrowding.

4. Divide the polenta between plates and arrange the roasted vegetables on top.

5. Garnish with fresh herbs and serve immediately.

Nutritional information (per portion)
Calories 300 kcal; Protein 6 g; Fat 10 g;
Sugar 6 g; Carbohydrates 45 g

PASTA WITH ROCKET PESTO

 Easy Portions 4 30 Minutes Vegan Gluten-free

INGREDIENTS

9 oz	chickpea pasta

FOR THE ROCKET PESTO

2 cups	fresh rocket, washed and dried
½ cup	walnuts (or pine nuts)
½ cup	olive oil
2	cloves of garlic, finely chopped

Juice of 1 lemon

Salt and freshly ground black pepper

TO SERVE

Fresh rocket leaves

Grated lemon zest

Optional: Yeast flakes for a cheesy flavor

PREPARATION

1. Cook the chickpea pasta in salted water according to the packet instructions until al dente. Drain and set aside.

2. For the rocket pesto, place the rocket, walnuts, olive oil, garlic, and lemon juice in a blender or food processor. Season with salt and pepper and purée to a smooth paste. For a creamier consistency, add more olive oil if required.

3. Place the cooked chickpea pasta in a large bowl and spread the rocket pesto over it. Stir well until all the pasta is evenly coated with the pesto.

4. Divide the pasta between plates and garnish with fresh rocket leaves, grated lemon zest, and optional yeast flakes.

Nutritional information (per portion)
Calories 450 kcal; Protein 20 g; Fat 25 g; Sugar 4 g; Carbohydrates 35 g

VEGETARIAN SOUP

Easy

Portions

50 Minutes

Vegan

Gluten-free

Nut-free

INGREDIENTS

1 tbsp	olive oil
1	large onion, diced
2	cloves of garlic, finely chopped
2	carrots, diced
2	stalks of celery, sliced
1	sweet potato, diced
1	small pumpkin (e.g., Hokkaido), diced
1 tsp	turmeric powder
½ tsp	ground ginger
¼ tsp	cayenne pepper (optional; adjust according to spiciness preference)
1 liter	vegetable stock (gluten-free)
1 tin	of chickpeas, rinsed and drained
2	handfuls of young spinach

Juice of 1 lemon

Salt and freshly ground black pepper

TO GARNISH

Fresh coriander or parsley

PREPARATION

1. In a large saucepan, heat the olive oil over medium heat. Add the onion, garlic, and sauté for 2–3 minutes until the onion is translucent.

2. Add the carrots, celery, sweet potato, and pumpkin. Stir in the turmeric powder, ground ginger, and cayenne pepper, and mix well. Cook for 5 minutes, stirring occasionally.

3. Add the vegetable stock and bring to a boil. Reduce the heat and simmer the soup for 20–25 minutes until the vegetables are soft.

4. Add the chickpeas and simmer for another 5 minutes.

5. Stir in the young spinach and lemon juice just before serving. Season to taste with salt and pepper.

6. Pour the soup into bowls and garnish with fresh coriander or parsley.

Nutritional information (per portion)
Calories 200 kcal; Protein 6 g; Fat 5 g;
Sugar 6 g; Carbohydrates 30 g

VEGETABLE CASSEROLE

 Easy **Portions** **1 Hour 10 Minutes** **Vegan** **Gluten-free** **Nut-free**

INGREDIENTS

1	medium sweet potato, cut into thin slices	2 tbsp	extra virgin olive oil
1	zucchini, cut into thin slices	2	cloves of garlic, finely chopped
1	eggplant, cut into thin slices	1 tsp	turmeric powder
1	red bell pepper, cut into strips	½ tsp	paprika powder
7 oz	cherry tomatoes, halved	¼ tsp	ground ginger
		Salt and freshly ground black pepper	

FOR THE SAUCE

1 ¾ cups of coconut milk

2 tbsp tomato purée

1 tsp turmeric powder

Salt and pepper to taste

TO GARNISH

Fresh herbs (e.g., parsley or coriander)

PREPARATION

1. Preheat the oven to 360 °F (180 °C).

2. Mix all the vegetable slices and strips in a large bowl with olive oil, chopped garlic, turmeric powder, paprika powder, ground ginger, salt, and pepper until evenly coated.

3. In a separate bowl, whisk together the coconut milk, tomato paste, turmeric powder, salt, and pepper to make the sauce.

4. Lightly grease a casserole dish with olive oil. Place the vegetable slices in the dish in layers, starting with the sweet potatoes, followed by the zucchini, eggplant, peppers, and cherry tomatoes.

5. Pour the coconut-tomato sauce evenly over the layered vegetables.

6. Bake the casserole in the preheated oven for about 45–50 minutes until the vegetables are tender, and the top appears lightly browned.

7. Garnish the vegetable casserole with fresh herbs before serving.

Nutritional information (per portion)
Calories 250 kcal; Protein 5 g; Fat 15 g;
Sugar 8 g; Carbohydrates 25 g

THAI VEGETABLE STEW

| Easy | Portions | 45 Minutes | Vegan | Gluten-free | Nut-free |

INGREDIENTS

1 tbsp	coconut oil
1 large	onion, finely diced
2	cloves of garlic, finely chopped
1	piece of fresh ginger, finely grated
1	red bell pepper, cut into strips
1	yellow bell pepper, cut into strips
1	zucchini, cut into half-moons
7 oz	cherry tomatoes, halved
7 oz	green beans, ends cut off and halved
1 ¾ cups	of coconut milk
4 cups	vegetable stock (gluten-free)
2 tbsp	tamari (gluten-free soy sauce)
1 tsp	turmeric powder

Juice of 1 lime

Fresh coriander to garnish

Salt and freshly ground black pepper

Optional: ½ tsp cayenne pepper

PREPARATION

1. In a large saucepan, heat coconut oil over medium heat. Add the onion, garlic, and ginger and sauté for 2–3 minutes until the onion is soft.

2. Add the red and yellow peppers, zucchini, cherry tomatoes, and green beans. Stir well and simmer for 5 minutes.

3. Add the coconut milk, vegetable stock, tamari, turmeric powder, and cayenne pepper. Bring to a boil, then reduce the heat and simmer gently for 20–25 minutes until the vegetables are soft.

4. Before serving, stir in the lime juice and season with salt and pepper to taste.

5. Pour the Thai vegetable stew into bowls and garnish with fresh coriander.

Nutritional information (per portion)
Calories 250 kcal; Protein 5 g; Fat 15 g;
Sugar 8 g; Carbohydrates 25 g

VEGETABLE CURRY

WITH QUINOA

 Easy
 Portions
 45 Minutes
 Vegan
 Gluten-free
 Nut-free

INGREDIENTS

FOR THE VEGETABLE CURRY

1 tbsp	coconut oil	14 oz	tin of chopped tomatoes
1	large onion, diced	1	sweet potato, diced
2	cloves of garlic, finely chopped	1	carrot, sliced
1	piece of fresh ginger (¾ inches), finely grated	1	red bell pepper, cut into strips
1 tsp	turmeric powder	7 oz	broccoli, cut into florets
½ tsp	ground coriander		Salt and freshly ground black pepper
½ tsp	ground cumin		
1 ¾ cups	of coconut milk		Optional: ¼ tsp cayenne pepper

FOR THE SIDE DISH

1 cup	quinoa, well rinsed	½ tsp	salt
2 cups	of water		

PREPARATION

1. Place the quinoa in a pan with water and salt. Bring to a boil, then reduce the heat, cover, and simmer for about 15–20 minutes until the quinoa is soft, and the water has been completely absorbed. Remove from the heat, cover, and leave to stand for 5 minutes.

2. Heat the coconut oil in a large saucepan over medium heat. Add the onion, garlic, and ginger and sauté for 2–3 minutes until the onion is soft.

3. Add the turmeric powder, coriander, cumin, and cayenne pepper and stir well.

4. Stir in the coconut milk and chopped tomatoes. Add the sweet potato, carrot, red bell pepper and broccoli. Bring to a boil, then reduce the heat and simmer the curry for about 20–25 minutes until the vegetables are soft.

5. Season to taste with salt and pepper.

6. Pour the vegetable curry over the cooked quinoa and serve.

Nutritional information (per serving)
Calories 450 kcal; Protein 12 g; Fat 20 g; Sugar 10 g; Carbohydrates 60 g

COCONUT MILK

———

Coconut milk is a valuable part of the anti-inflammatory diet thanks to lauric acid, which boosts the immune system and has an anti-inflammatory effect. Its antioxidants help reduce oxidative damage. As a dairy-free alternative, it enriches numerous dishes with its creamy texture. Despite its health benefits, coconut milk should be consumed in moderation due to its saturated fat content, but it fits nicely into a balanced, plant-based diet.

HERB OMELETTE

 Easy   **Portions**   **15 Minutes**   **Vegetarian**   **Lactose-free**   **Gluten-free**   **Nut-free**

INGREDIENTS

4	large organic eggs
1 tbsp	extra virgin olive oil
¼ cup	chopped fresh herbs (basil, parsley, dill)
1	small onion, finely diced

1	clove of garlic, finely chopped

Salt and freshly ground black pepper to taste

A pinch of turmeric

Optional. A pinch of cayenne pepper (optional)

PREPARATION

1. Wash the herbs, shake them dry, and chop finely. Peel and finely dice the onion and garlic.

2. Break the eggs into a bowl and whisk lightly. Add the chopped herbs, turmeric, and a pinch of cayenne pepper (if using). Season with salt and pepper and mix well.

3. Heat the olive oil in a non-stick frying pan over medium heat. Add the onion and garlic and sauté, stirring, until softened but not browned, about 2–3 minutes.

4. Pour the egg mixture over the sautéed onions and garlic in the pan. Turn the heat low and allow the omelette to set slowly until the surface is almost firm. Use a spatula to carefully lift the edges, so the liquid egg mixture can flow underneath.

5. Once the omelette is almost cooked, carefully flip it over with a wide spatula and cook on the other side for 1–2 minutes.

6. Slide the omelette onto a plate and serve immediately. Garnish with additional fresh herbs if desired.

HERBS

Herbs such as turmeric, ginger, rosemary, and thyme are vital components of an anti-inflammatory diet. They contain powerful antioxidants and phytochemicals that reduce inflammation in the body and boost the immune system. Regular use of herbs in the kitchen can help fight chronic inflammation and promote overall health, while adding flavor and aroma to dishes.

Nutritional information (per portion)
Calories 250 kcal; Protein 16 g;
Fat 18 g ; Carbohydrates 4 g

LENTIL SALAD

WITH ROASTED VEGETABLES

Easy **Portions** **40 Minutes** **Vegan** **Gluten-free** **Nut-free**

INGREDIENTS

FOR THE SALAD

1 cup	green lentils, well rinsed		**1**	yellow bell pepper, cut into strips
1	medium-sized zucchini, cut into half-moons		**1 tbsp**	olive oil
1	red bell pepper, cut into strips			Salt and freshly ground black pepper
				A few leaves of fresh spinach

FOR THE DRESSING

3 tbsp	extra virgin olive oil		**1 tsp**	freshly grated ginger
1 tsp	turmeric powder			Juice of 1 large lemon
½ tsp	ground cumin			

PREPARATION

1. Place the lentils in a pan with plenty of water and bring to a boil. Reduce the heat and simmer for about 20–25 minutes until soft but firm to the bite. Drain and leave to cool.

2. Heat the olive oil in a frying pan over medium heat. Add the zucchini and peppers, and season with salt and pepper. Fry for about 8–10 minutes, stirring occasionally, until the vegetables are soft and lightly browned. Remove from the heat and allow to cool.

3. In a small bowl, mix together the olive oil, lemon juice, turmeric, cumin and ginger. Season with salt and pepper and mix thoroughly until a homogeneous mixture is obtained.

4. In a large salad bowl, gently mix the cooked lentils, roasted vegetables, and fresh spinach leaves. Pour the prepared dressing over the salad and mix well.

5. Arrange the lentil salad on plates and serve immediately, or keep it in the fridge for later. Recheck the dressing just before serving and season if necessary.

Nutritional information (per portion)
Calories 350 kcal; Protein 15 g; Fat 14 g;
Sugar 6 g; Carbohydrates 45 g

CAULIFLOWER PIZZA

 Medium   **Portions** (4)   **45 Minutes**   **Vegan**   **Gluten-free**   **Nut-free**

INGREDIENTS

1	medium cauliflower (about 20 oz), cut into florets
2 tbsp	ground linseed mixed with 6 tbsp water (as an egg substitute)
½ cup	almond flour
1 tsp	garlic powder
1 tsp	dried oregano
2 tbsp	olive oil
1 tin	of strained tomatoes (without additives)
1 tsp	dried basil
1	small red onion, thinly sliced
½	red bell pepper, cut into thin strips
½	yellow bell pepper, cut into thin strips

A few fresh basil leaves for decoration

Salt and freshly ground black pepper to taste

PREPARATION

1. Finely grind cauliflower florets in a food processor until a rice grain-like texture is achieved. Transfer the ground cauliflower to a microwave-safe bowl, cover it, and cook for 5 minutes on high power. Leave to cool.

2. Transfer the pre-cooked cauliflower to a clean kitchen towel and squeeze out as much water as possible.

3. In a large bowl, combine the squeezed cauliflower, ground linseed, and the linseed water mixture, along with almond flour, garlic powder, oregano, salt, and pepper. Knead well until a compact mass is formed.

4. Preheat the oven to 400 °F (200 °C). Line a baking tray with baking paper and place the cauliflower mixture on it. Shape into a round pizza base about 1 cm thick with your hands. Brush with olive oil and bake in the preheated oven for about 20 minutes until the edges are golden.

5. Season the tomato purée with basil, salt and pepper. Remove the pizza base from the oven and spread the tomato sauce on top. Top with red onion slices and red and yellow bell pepper strips.

6. Return the pizza to the oven and bake for an additional 10–15 minutes until the vegetables are tender.

7. Garnish with fresh basil leaves before serving.

Nutritional information (per portion)
Calories 320 kcal; Protein 10 g; Fat 20 g;
Sugar 10 g; Carbohydrates 30 g

SIDE DISHES AND SAUCES

HUMMUS

 Easy

 Portions

 15 Minutes

 Vegan

 Gluten-free

INGREDIENTS

1 tin	(14 oz) chickpeas, rinsed and drained	**½ tsp**	cumin
2 tbsp	tahini (sesame paste)	Salt and freshly ground black pepper to taste	
2	cloves of garlic, finely chopped	A few leaves of fresh coriander or parsley to garnish	
2 tbsp	olive oil	Juice of 1 lemon	

PREPARATION

1. Thoroughly rinse and drain the chickpeas. For an even smoother hummus, remove the skin from the chickpeas by gently squeezing each chickpea between your thumb and forefinger.

2. Place the drained chickpeas in a large bowl and mash with a potato masher or the back of a fork until you have a coarse paste.

3. Add the tahini, finely chopped garlic, lemon juice, olive oil, and cumin. Stir in optional cayenne pepper for a slightly spicy note. Season with salt and pepper to taste.

4. Mix all ingredients thoroughly and continue to mash until the mixture is as smooth as possible. For a finer consistency, stir in a little water or olive oil until the desired consistency is achieved.

5. Taste the hummus and adjust the seasoning if necessary. Transfer to a serving bowl, make a well in the center with a spoon, and pour in additional olive oil. Garnish with fresh herbs such as coriander or parsley.

Nutritional information (per portion)
Calories 150 kcal; Protein 6 g; Fat 10 g;
Sugar 6 g; Carbohydrates 12 g

GUACAMOLE

 Easy   **Portions** 6   **10 Minutes**   **Vegan**   **Gluten-free**   **Nut-free**

INGREDIENTS

2	ripe avocados, halved, pitted and peeled
2 tbsp	finely chopped red onion
1	clove of garlic, finely chopped
½	red bell pepper, finely diced
¼ tsp	ground turmeric

Juice of 1 lime

Salt and freshly ground black pepper to taste

Fresh coriander, chopped, to garnish

Optional: ¼ tsp ground cayenne pepper

PREPARATION

1. Place the avocados in a bowl and mash with a fork until the desired consistency is achieved. Some like it chunky, others creamier.

2. Add lime juice, finely chopped red onion, garlic, red bell pepper, turmeric, and cayenne pepper (if using). Season with salt and pepper to taste.

3. Mix all the ingredients thoroughly until a homogeneous mixture is formed.

4. Place the guacamole in a serving bowl and garnish with fresh coriander. Serve immediately to prevent it from browning. A tip to keep the guacamole fresh is to leave the avocado pit in the bowl until ready to serve.

Nutritional information (per serving)
Calories 160 kcal; Protein 2 g; Fat 14 g; Sugar 1 g; Carbohydrates 10 g

HERB DIP

 Easy   Portions   15 Minutes   Vegan   Gluten-free   Nut-free

INGREDIENTS

1 cup	coconut yogurt (unsweetened)
¼ cup	fresh dill, finely chopped
¼ cup	fresh parsley, finely chopped
2 tbsp	fresh chives, finely chopped
1 tbsp	extra virgin olive oil
2 tsp	fresh lemon juice
1	small clove of garlic, finely chopped
¼ tsp	ground turmeric

Salt and freshly ground black pepper to taste

PREPARATION

1. Wash, dry, and finely chop the dill, parsley, and chives.

2. Peel and finely chop the garlic clove.

3. In a medium bowl, add the coconut yogurt, olive oil, lemon juice, chopped garlic, turmeric, salt and pepper. Mix everything well.

4. Add the chopped herbs to the bowl and fold in thoroughly until well combined.

5. Taste the dip and season with salt, pepper, or lemon juice if necessary. Transfer to a serving bowl and serve as a side dish with vegetable sticks, wholemeal crackers, or a healthy sauce with grilled vegetables or meat.

Nutritional information (per portion)
Calories 70 kcal; Protein 2 g; Fat 5 g;
Sugar 3 g; Carbohydrates 4 g

PUMPKIN SALAD

WITH POMEGRANATE

Easy

Portions

40 Minutes

Vegan

Gluten-free

Nut-free

INGREDIENTS

1	small Hokkaido pumpkin, deseeded and cut into 1 cm thick slices
2 tbsp	olive oil
1 tsp	ground cinnamon
½ tsp	ground turmeric
3.5 oz	baby spinach
1	medium pome-granate, seeded
2 oz	pine nuts, lightly roasted
2 tbsp	apple cider vinegar
1 tbsp	maple syrup
1 tbsp	freshly squeezed orange juice

Salt and freshly ground black pepper

The zest of 1 organic orange, finely grated

PREPARATION

1. Preheat the oven to 400 °F (200 °C). Place the pumpkin slices on a baking tray lined with baking paper and drizzle with olive oil. Sprinkle with cinnamon, turmeric, salt, and pepper and mix well. Roast in the oven for approx. 25–30 minutes until the pumpkin is soft and slightly caramelized around the edges.

2. Meanwhile, in a small bowl, whisk together the balsamic vinegar, maple syrup, orange juice, and orange zest to make a dressing. Season to taste with salt and pepper.

3. Spread out the baby spinach on a large serving platter. Spread the roasted pumpkin on top and sprinkle with pome-granate seeds and pine nuts.

4. Drizzle the dressing evenly over the salad. Stir gently before serving to combine the flavors.

Nutritional information (per portion)
Calories 200 kcal; Protein 4 g; Fat 10 g;
Sugar 12 g; Carbohydrates 25 g

OVEN VEGETABLES

WITH TAHINI SAUCE

 Easy   Portions   45 Minutes   Vegan   Gluten-free

INGREDIENTS

FOR THE VEGETABLES

1	medium-sized sweet potato, diced
2	carrots, cut into slices
1	red bell pepper, cut into strips

1	broccoli, cut into florets
2 tbsp	extra virgin olive oil

Salt and freshly ground black pepper to taste

FOR THE TAHINI SAUCE

1/4 cup	tahini (sesame paste)
2 tbsp	lemon juice
1 tbsp	extra virgin olive oil
1	small clove of garlic, finely chopped

1/4 tsp	ground turmeric

Water, as required for the desired consistency

Salt and freshly ground black pepper to taste

PREPARATION

1. Preheat your oven to 200°C (400°F).

2. In a large bowl, combine the diced vegetables. Drizzle with 2 tablespoons of extra virgin olive oil, and season with salt and black pepper.

3. Spread the seasoned vegetables in a single layer on a baking sheet lined with parchment paper. Roast in the preheated oven for 25-30 minutes, or until the vegetables are tender and slightly caramelized, stirring halfway through the cooking time for even roasting.

4. While the vegetables are roasting, prepare the tahini sauce. In a small bowl, combine the tahini, lemon juice, 1 tablespoon of extra virgin olive oil, finely chopped garlic, and ground turmeric. Gradually add water until the sauce reaches your desired consistency. Season with salt and pepper.

5. Once the vegetables are done roasting, remove them from the oven and transfer to a serving dish. Drizzle the tahini sauce over the roasted vegetables or serve it on the side as a dipping sauce.

Nutritional information (per serving)
Calories 200 kcal; Protein 4 g; Fat 14 g;
Sugar 5 g; Carbohydrates 18 g

AVOCADO AND LENTIL SALAD

WITH LEMON DRESSING

 Easy

 4 Portions

 20 Minutes

 Vegan

 Gluten-free

 Nut-free

INGREDIENTS

7 oz	green lentils, pre-cooked
1	ripe avocado, diced
7 oz	cherry tomatoes, halved
3.5 oz	rocket salad
1	small red onion, finely diced
2 tbsp	extra virgin olive oil
1 tsp	Dijon mustard

Juice and zest of 1 organic lemon

Salt and freshly ground black pepper

A few fresh basil leaves to garnish

PREPARATION

1. Place the pre-cooked lentils in a large salad bowl.

2. Add the diced avocado, halved cherry tomatoes, rocket, and diced red onion to the lentils.

3. In a small bowl, whisk together the olive oil, lemon juice, zest, Dijon mustard, salt, and pepper to make a dressing.

4. Pour the dressing over the salad and stir gently to mix and marinate the ingredients evenly.

5. Arrange the salad on plates and garnish with fresh basil leaves.

LEMON

Lemon is a powerhouse in anti-inflammatory nutrition, rich in vitamin C and antioxidants that boost the immune system and protect against free radicals. Its high content of antioxidant flavonoids has an anti-inflammatory effect and supports liver function. Regularly including lemon water or freshly squeezed lemon juice in meals can improve iron absorption from plant sources and promote overall health.

Nutritional information (per portion)
Calories 250 kcal; Protein 9 g; Fat 14 g;
Sugar 3 g; Carbohydrates 23 g

BRAISED FENNEL

WITH ORANGES AND OLIVES

 Easy   **Portions**   **40 Minutes**   **Vegan**   **Gluten-free**   **Nut-free**

INGREDIENTS

4	medium-sized fennel bulbs, quartered	¼ cup	black olives, pitted
2 tbsp	olive oil	1 tsp	dried thyme
2	oranges, one sliced, the other squeezed	Salt and freshly ground black pepper	

PREPARATION

1. Preheat the oven to 360 °F (180 °C). Line a large baking tray with baking paper.

2. Spread the fennel quarters on the baking tray and drizzle with olive oil. Season with salt and pepper and mix well.

3. Arrange the orange slices between the fennel pieces. Cook the fennel in the preheated oven for about 30 minutes until it is soft and slightly caramelized around the edges.

4. Meanwhile, mix the orange juice, olives, and thyme in a small bowl.

5. Remove the fennel pieces from the oven and pour the orange and olive mixture over the hot fennel. Stir everything carefully so that the fennel is evenly coated with the mixture.

6. Leave in the oven for a few minutes before serving to allow the flavors to combine.

Nutritional information (per portion)
Calories 120 kcal; Protein 2 g; Fat 7 g;
Sugar 8 g; Carbohydrates 12 g

ROASTED CHICKPEAS

Easy

Portions

40 Minutes

Vegan

Gluten-free

Nut-free

INGREDIENTS

1 tin (14 oz) chickpeas, rinsed and drained

2 tbsp extra virgin olive oil

1 tsp turmeric powder

½ tsp ground cumin

½ tsp paprika powder

Salt and freshly ground black pepper to taste

Optional: ¼ tsp cayenne pepper

PREPARATION

1. Rinse chickpeas thoroughly and pat dry with kitchen paper. Remove as much moisture as possible for a crispy texture.

2. Place the dried chickpeas in a bowl and drizzle with olive oil. Add the turmeric, cumin, cayenne pepper (if using), paprika powder, salt and pepper.

3. Mix everything well so that the chickpeas are evenly coated with the spices.

4. Preheat the oven to 400 °F (200 °C).

5. Spread the spiced chickpeas on a baking tray lined with baking paper so they are in a single layer.

6. Roast in the oven for about 30–35 minutes until golden brown and crispy. Halfway through the baking time, turn the chickpeas once to ensure even roasting.

7. Remove the roasted chickpeas from the oven and allow to cool slightly. They will become even crispier as they cool.

8. Serve as a healthy snack or a crunchy side dish for salads and bowls.

Nutritional information (per portion)
Calories 150 kcal; Protein 7 g; Fat 7 g;
Sugar 5 g; Carbohydrates 18 g

ROASTED
BRUSSELS SPROUTS

WITH POMEGRANATE AND WALNUTS

| Easy | Portions | 25 Minutes | Vegan | Gluten-free |

INGREDIENTS

. . . .

18 oz	Brussels sprouts, cleaned and halved	2 tsp	maple syrup
		1 tbsp	apple cider vinegar
2 tbsp	olive oil		
½	pomegranate, seeds removed	Salt and freshly ground black pepper	
2 oz	walnuts, roughly chopped	A few fresh thyme leaves	

PREPARATION

. . . .

1. Preheat the oven to 400 °F (200 °C). Line a baking tray with baking paper.

2. Spread the Brussels sprouts halves on the baking tray and drizzle with olive oil. Season with salt and pepper. Mix well to ensure the Brussels sprouts are evenly coated with the oil.

3. Roast the Brussels sprouts in the preheated oven for 20 minutes until golden brown and tender, turning once to ensure even browning.

4. While the Brussels sprouts are roasting, toast the walnuts in a dry frying pan over medium heat for a few minutes until fragrant. Set aside.

5. Remove the roasted Brussels sprouts from the oven and place them in a serving bowl. Drizzle with maple syrup and balsamic vinegar and stir gently.

6. Sprinkle with pomegranate seeds and toasted walnuts. Garnish with fresh thyme leaves and serve.

Nutritional information (per portion)
Calories 200 kcal; Protein 5 g; Fat 14 g;
Sugar 7 g; Carbohydrates 16 g

SWEET POTATO FRIES

 Easy
 Portions
 10 Minutes & Baking 25-30 Minutes
 Vegan
 Gluten-free
 Nut-free

INGREDIENTS

2	large sweet potatoes, peeled and cut into fries
2 tbsp	olive oil
1 tsp	paprika powder
½ tsp	turmeric powder
¼ tsp	garlic powder
¼ tsp	cinnamon

Salt and black pepper to taste

Optional: A pinch of cayenne pepper

PREPARATION

1. Preheat your oven to 430 °F (220 °C) and line a baking tray with baking paper.

2. In a large bowl, mix the sweet potato fries with olive oil, paprika powder, turmeric, garlic powder, cinnamon, cayenne pepper (if using), salt and pepper until all the fries are evenly coated.

3. Spread the seasoned sweet potato fries in a single layer on the prepared baking sheet. Make sure they are not on top of each other to ensure optimum crispiness.

4. Bake the fries for about 25–30 minutes, or until crispy around the edges and cooked through. Turn them halfway through baking to ensure even browning.

5. Remove the sweet potato fries from the oven and allow them to cool for a few minutes before serving. Optionally, you can sprinkle them with fresh herbs such as parsley or serve with an anti-inflammatory dip such as an avocado or tahini dip.

Nutritional information (per serving)
Calories 200 kcal; Protein 2 g; Fat 7 g; Sugar 10 g; Carbohydrates 33 g

DESSERTS

OAT COOKIES

WITH BANANA AND CINNAMON

Easy

12 Cookies

25 Minutes

Vegan

Gluten-free
(optional)

Nut-free

INGREDIENTS

2	ripe bananas, mashed	1 tsp	cinnamon
1 cup	rolled oats (glutenfree, if necessary)	1 tbsp	linseed, ground
		1 tbsp	chia seeds
¼ cup	raisins	¼ tsp	salt

PREPARATION

1. Preheat the oven to 360 °F (180 °C) and line a baking tray with baking paper.

2. In a large bowl, mix the mashed bananas, rolled oats, raisins, cinnamon, ground linseed, chia seeds, and salt until they are well combined.

3. Using a tablespoon, place small mounds of dough on the baking tray and flatten slightly to form the cookie shape.

4. Bake the cookies in the preheated oven for about 15–18 minutes until they are firm and lightly browned.

5. Allow the cookies to cool completely on a cooling rack before serving.

CINNAMON

Cinnamon, a popular spice with a sweet and spicy flavor, is also known for its anti-inflammatory properties. It contains antioxidants such as cinnamaldehyde, which can reduce inflammation and improve insulin sensitivity, making it particularly valuable for people with blood sugar problems. Regularly using cinnamon in the diet can enhance dishes, help protect against chronic diseases, and support general well-being.

Nutritional information (per serving)
Calories 90 kcal; Protein 2 g; Fat 1.5 g;
Sugar 5 g; Carbohydrates 17 g

BERRY MUFFINS

 Easy   12 Muffins   35 Minutes   Vegan   Gluten-free   Nut-free

INGREDIENTS

1 ½ cups gluten-free flour (e.g., oat flour, buckwheat flour, or almond flour)

½ cup almond milk

¼ cup coconut oil, melted

½ cup maple syrup

1 tsp vanilla extract

1 tsp baking powder

½ tsp baking soda

¼ tsp salt

1 cup mixed berries (fresh or frozen)

PREPARATION

1. Preheat the oven to 360 °F (180 °C) and line a muffin tray with paper cases or grease with some oil.

2. Mix the gluten-free flour, baking powder, baking soda, and salt in a large bowl.

3. In another bowl, whisk together the almond milk, melted coconut oil, maple syrup, and vanilla extract.

4. Add the wet ingredients to the dry ingredients and stir gently until just combined.

5. Carefully fold in the berries.

6. Divide the batter evenly between the muffin tins so that each tin is about two-thirds full.

7. Bake in the preheated oven for about 20–25 minutes, or until a toothpick comes out clean.

8. Allow the muffins to cool in the tray for 5 minutes, then transfer to a cooling rack to cool completely.

FROZEN OR FRESH?

The decision between fresh and frozen food depends on availability and preference. Fresh food is available straight from the harvest but can lose nutrients if it is transported or stored for a long time. Frozen foods are flash-frozen shortly after harvest, which preserves nutrients and extends shelf life. Both options can be nutrient-rich, but healthy preparation is important.

Nutritional information (per serving)
Calories 150 kcal; Protein 2 g; Fat 5 g;
Sugar 8 g; Carbohydrates 22 g

AVOCADO CHOCOLATE MOUSSE

Easy

Portions

15 Minutes

Vegan

Gluten-free

Nut-free

INGREDIENTS

2	ripe avocados, peeled and pitted	½ tsp	vanilla extract
¼ cup	cocoa powder, unsweetened	1	pinch of salt
¼ cup	maple syrup or honey to taste	**Optional** for additional sweetness: 1-2 tbsp agave syrup	

PREPARATION

1. Place the peeled and pitted avocados in a blender together with the cocoa powder, maple syrup, vanilla extract, and a pinch of salt.

2. Blend until smooth and creamy. If necessary, add agave syrup to increase the sweetness.

3. Pour the mousse into dessert bowls and chill for at least 1 hour to set.

4. Before serving, the mousse can be garnished with fresh berries or a mint leaf.

Nutritional information (per serving)
Calories 250 kcal; Protein 3 g; Fat 15 g;
Sugar 12 g; Carbohydrates 30 g

DARK CHOCOLATE QUINOA BALLS

Easy

Portions

30 Minutes

Vegan

Gluten-free

Nut-free
(optional)

INGREDIENTS

6 oz	cooked quinoa, cooled
½ cup	coconut oil, melted
1 oz	cocoa powder, unsweetened
¼ cup	maple syrup
1 tsp	vanilla extract
1	pinch of salt

2 oz   dark chocolate (at least 70% cocoa content), finely chopped

Optional: 1 oz chopped nuts

PREPARATION

1. Cook the quinoa according to the instructions and leave to cool.

2. In a medium bowl, mix the cooled quinoa, melted coconut oil, cocoa powder, maple syrup, vanilla extract, and a pinch of salt until well combined.

3. Add the finely chopped dark chocolate (and the chopped nuts, if preferred) and mix thoroughly again.

4. Place the mixture in the fridge for about 10 minutes until slightly firm, making it easier to shape the balls.

5. Scoop out small portions of the mixture with a spoon and shape into balls with your hands. Place on a baking tray lined with baking paper.

6. Place the quinoa balls in the fridge for at least 20 minutes to firm up.

7. The balls can be stored in an airtight container in the fridge.

Nutritional information (per portion)
Calories 150 kcal; Protein 2 g; Fat 10 g; Sugar 6 g; Carbohydrates 15 g

BERRY CRISP

Easy

4
Portions

35 Minutes

Vegan

Gluten-free

Nut-free
(optional)

INGREDIENTS

FOR THE FILLING

18 oz	mixed berries (fresh or frozen)
1 tbsp	chia seeds
2 tbsp	maple syrup
1 tsp	vanilla extract
½ tsp	ground cinnamon

FOR THE CRUMBLE

3.5 oz	rolled oats (gluten-free)
2 oz	ground almonds (for a Nut-free version, use additional rolled oats instead)
2 tbsp	maple syrup
2 tbsp	coconut oil, melted
½ tsp	ground cinnamon

PREPARATION

1. Preheat the oven to 360 °F (180 °C) and lightly grease a baking dish with coconut oil.

2. Mix the berries, chia seeds, maple syrup, vanilla extract, and cinnamon in a bowl. Spread the berry mixture evenly in the prepared baking dish.

3. In another bowl, combine the rolled oats, ground almonds (or additional rolled oats), maple syrup, melted coconut oil, and cinnamon to make a crumble mixture. Sprinkle this mixture evenly over the berries in the baking dish.

4. Place the baking dish in the preheated oven and bake for about 25 minutes until the crumble is golden brown and the berry mixture starts to bubble.

5. Remove the berry crisp from the oven and leave to cool briefly before serving. Optionally, the dessert can be served with a scoop of Lactose-free vanilla ice cream or coconut yogurt.

Nutritional information (per serving)
Calories 250 kcal; Protein 4 g; Fat 10 g;
Sugar 15 g; Carbohydrates 35 g

BERRY ICE CREAM

 Easy
 4 Portions
 120 Minutes incl. freezing time
 Vegan
 Gluten-free
 Nut-free

INGREDIENTS

10.5 oz mixed berries (fresh or frozen)

2 tbsp maple syrup

1 ⅔ cups coconut milk (full-fat, well chilled)

1 tsp vanilla extract

PREPARATION

1. Place the mixed berries in a bowl and mix with maple syrup.

2. Pour the coconut milk into another bowl. It is important that the coconut milk is well chilled so that the solid part separates from the watery part.

3. Using a hand mixer, beat the coconut milk with the vanilla extract until stiff and creamy.

4. Carefully fold the berry mixture into the coconut milk cream to achieve a marbled appearance.

5. Pour the mixture into a freezer-safe container and freeze for at least 2 hours, or until firm.

6. Leave the berry ice cream at room temperature for a few minutes before serving to facilitate scooping.

Nutritional information (per portion)
Calories 150 kcal; Protein 1.5 g; Fat 10 g; Sugar 8 g; Carbohydrates 12 g

VANILLA PUDDING

| Easy | Portions | 15 Minutes | Vegan | Gluten-free | Nut-free |

INGREDIENTS

2 cups almond milk (unsweetened)

1.4 oz cornstarch

2 ⅔ tbsp maple syrup

2 tsp vanilla extract

A pinch of turmeric (for the color)

PREPARATION

1. In a medium saucepan, heat 4/5 of the almond milk, maple syrup, and a pinch of turmeric over medium heat. Do not bring it to a boil.

2. Whisk the remaining 1/5 of almond milk with the cornstarch in a small bowl until there are no lumps.

3. Slowly add the cornstarch mixture to the warmed almond milk, stirring constantly.

4. Continue to heat the mixture, stirring constantly, until it thickens and starts to bubble. Then, remove from the heat.

5. Stir in the vanilla extract and transfer the mixture to dessert bowls or a large container.

6. Allow the pudding to cool slightly at room temperature, then place in the fridge to cool completely. The pudding will continue to thicken as it cools.

7. Garnish with fresh berries or a pinch of cinnamon as desired before serving.

Nutritional information (per serving)
Calories 120 kcal; Protein 1 g; Fat 2.5 g;
Sugar 6 g; Carbohydrates 20 g

BERRY SORBET

WITH MINT

Easy

Portions

10 Minutes
incl. freezing time

Vegan

Gluten-free

Nut-free

INGREDIENTS

18 oz mixed berries (fresh or frozen)

½ cup maple syrup

2 tbsp freshly squeezed lemon juice

A few leaves of fresh mint

PREPARATION

1. Place the berries, maple syrup, lemon juice, and mint in a high-powered blender.

2. Blend everything at high speed until the mixture is smooth.

3. Pass the mixture through a fine sieve to remove the seeds and obtain a smooth sorbet base.

4. Pour the sorbet base into a freezer-safe mold and freeze for at least 4 hours or overnight until the sorbet is firm.

5. Leave the sorbet at room temperature for about 10 minutes to thaw slightly before serving. Then, use an ice cream scoop to form balls.

6. Divide the sorbet into bowls and garnish with fresh mint leaves.

Nutritional information (per serving)
Calories 150 kcal; Protein 1 g; Fat 0.5 g;
Sugar 20 g; Carbohydrates 36 g

CHOCOLATE BARK

 Easy   **4** **Portions**   **15 Minutes** + cooling time   **Vegan**   **Gluten-free**

INGREDIENTS

7 oz	dark chocolate (at least 70% cocoa, sugar-free)
2 tbsp	coconut oil
¼ cup	chopped almonds
¼ cup	chopped walnuts
2 tbsp	goji berries
1 tsp	chia seeds
¼ cup	pumpkin seeds

A pinch of sea salt

PREPARATION

1. Melt the dark chocolate with coconut oil in a bain-marie or microwave until it is entirely liquid. Stir constantly to ensure even melting.

2. Pour the melted chocolate mixture onto a baking tray lined with baking paper and spread evenly with a spatula until a thin layer is formed.

3. Sprinkle the chopped almonds, walnuts, goji berries, chia, and pumpkin seeds evenly over the still-liquid chocolate. Sprinkle with a pinch of sea salt.

4. Place the baking tray in the fridge for at least 2 hours until the chocolate has set.

5. Once the chocolate is hard, break it or cut it into irregular pieces.

6. Keep the Chocolate Bark in the fridge until ready to eat.

Nutritional information (per serving)
Calories 200 kcal; Protein 3 g; Fat 15 g;
Sugar 2 g; Carbohydrates 10 g

CHOCOLATE BANANA MUFFINS

 Easy   **Muffins**   **35 Minutes**   **Vegan**   **Gluten-free**

INGREDIENTS

7 oz	almond flour	**5 tbsp**	maple syrup or another natural sweetener
2 oz	cocoa powder, unsweetened	**1/4 cup**	melted coconut oil
1 tsp	baking powder (gluten-free)	**1 tsp**	vanilla extract
1/4 tsp	sea salt	**1/4 cup**	almond milk
3	ripe bananas, mashed	**3.5 oz**	dark chocolate chips (at least 70% cocoa, sugar-free)

PREPARATION

1. Preheat the oven to 360 °F (180 °C). Line a muffin tin with paper cases or grease with a little coconut oil.

2. In a large bowl, mix the almond flour, cocoa powder, baking powder, and sea salt.

3. In a separate bowl, mix the mashed bananas, maple syrup, melted coconut oil, vanilla extract, and almond milk.

4. Add the wet ingredients to the dry ingredients and mix well until a smooth batter forms. Fold in the dark chocolate chips.

5. Pour the batter evenly into the prepared muffin tins.

6. Bake the muffins for about 20–25 minutes, or until a toothpick comes out clean.

7. Remove from the oven and allow to cool completely before serving.

Nutritional information (per muffin)
Calories 220 kcal; Protein 5 g; Fat 14 g;
Sugar 8 g; Carbohydrates 18 g

SNACKS

SPICY WAFFLES

Medium   Portions   30 Minutes   Vegetarian   Gluten-free   Nut-free   Lactose-free

INGREDIENTS

7 oz	buckwheat flour	1	red bell pepper, finely diced
1 tsp	baking powder (gluten-free)	2 tbsp	fresh parsley, finely chopped
¼ tsp	turmeric		Salt and freshly ground black pepper
¼ tsp	paprika powder		
2	organic eggs		A little over 3 tbsp extra virgin olive oil
1 ¼ cups	almond milk		
			Coconut oil for the waffle iron
1	small zucchini, finely grated		

PREPARATION

1. Preheat a waffle iron and lightly grease with coconut oil.

2. Mix the buckwheat flour, baking powder, sea salt, turmeric, and paprika powder in a large bowl.

3. In another bowl, beat the eggs with the almond milk and olive oil until frothy. Add this mixture to the dry ingredients and stir well until you have a smooth batter.

4. Fold the zucchini, red bell pepper, and parsley into the batter and thoroughly mix everything.

5. Pour the batter into the preheated waffle iron in batches and bake the waffles until golden brown. Each waffle should bake for about 5–7 minutes, depending on the waffle iron.

6. Serve the finished waffles warm. They go perfectly with fresh salads or as a hearty breakfast.

Nutritional information (per portion)
Calories 250 kcal; Protein 6 g; Fat 14 g;
Sugar 2 g; Carbohydrates 25 g

SPICY NUTS

Easy   Portions   25 Minutes   Vegan   Gluten-free

INGREDIENTS

7 oz	raw, mixed nuts (e.g., almonds, walnuts, pecans, etc.)
1 tbsp	olive oil
1/2 tsp	ground turmeric
1/4 tsp	paprika powder

Salt and freshly ground black pepper

PREPARATION

1. Preheat the oven to 360 °F (180 °C). Line a baking tray with baking paper.

2. Mix the nuts in a bowl with the olive oil until all the nuts are slightly oily.

3. Mix the sea salt, black pepper, turmeric, paprika, and cayenne pepper in a small bowl and sprinkle over the nuts. Mix everything thoroughly so that the spices are evenly distributed.

4. Spread the seasoned nuts on the prepared baking sheet in a single layer.

5. Roast the nuts in the preheated oven for 10–15 minutes, or until golden brown and fragrant. Turn once in between to ensure they toast evenly.

6. Remove the nuts from the oven and leave to cool completely. They will become crispier as they cool.

Nutritional information (per serving)
Calories 150 kcal; Protein 4 g; Fat 13 g;
Sugar 1 g; Carbohydrates 6 g

BAKED TURMERIC CHICKPEAS

Easy

Portions

40 Minutes

Vegan

Gluten-free

Nut-free

INGREDIENTS

14 oz	chickpeas (drained weight) from the tin, rinsed and dried
1 tbsp	extra virgin olive oil
½ tsp	ground turmeric
¼ tsp	ground ginger
¼ tsp	paprika powder

A pinch of cayenne pepper

Salt and freshly ground black pepper to taste

PREPARATION

1. Preheat the oven to 400 °F (200 °C) and line a baking tray with baking paper.

2. Place the rinsed and thoroughly dried chickpeas in a bowl and mix evenly with the olive oil.

3. Add the turmeric, ginger, paprika, cayenne pepper, salt, and pepper and mix well until the chickpeas are evenly seasoned.

4. Spread the seasoned chickpeas on the prepared baking sheet and bake for about 25–30 minutes, or until golden brown and crispy. Turn once halfway through to ensure even browning.

5. Allow the baked turmeric chickpeas to cool slightly, and enjoy it as an energy-boosting, anti-inflammatory snack.

Nutritional information (per serving)
Calories 150 kcal; Protein 7 g; Fat 5 g;
Sugar 3 g; Carbohydrates 20 g

BLUEBERRY CASHEW SHAKE

 Easy   **Shake**   **10 Minutes**   **Vegan**   **Gluten-free**

INGREDIENTS

1 cup	frozen blueberries
1/4 cup	cashews, soaked overnight and rinsed
2 tbsp	chia seeds
1 tbsp	linseed
1/2 tsp	cinnamon

1 tsp	pure vanilla extract
1 cup	unsweetened almond milk
1 tbsp	coconut oil

Optional: 1 tbsp honey or maple syrup for extra sweetness (only if allowed in your diet)

PREPARATION

1. Soak cashews in water for at least 4 hours or overnight. Rinse and drain before use.

2. Place all ingredients in a high-powered blender.

3. Blend on high speed until the mixture is smooth and creamy. This may take a few minutes, depending on the power of your blender.

4. Taste and sweeten with honey or maple syrup if required.

5. Serve immediately and enjoy. Add a few ice cubes while blending for an extra cool refreshment.

Nutritional information (per serving)
Calories 280 kcal; Protein 7 g; Fat 19 g;
Sugar 15 g; Carbohydrates 24 g (without optional sweetener)

BANANA BREAD

Easy

Bread

**1 Hour
10 Minutes**

Vegan

Gluten-free

INGREDIENTS

3	ripe bananas, mashed	**½ tsp**	salt
¼ cup	coconut oil, melted	**¾ tsp**	baking powder
¼ cup	maple syrup	**½ tsp**	cinnamon
2 tsp	vanilla extract	**¼ cup**	chopped walnuts (optional)
2 cups	gluten-free oat flour	**¼ cup**	unsweetened almond milk

PREPARATION

1. Preheat the oven to 360 °F (180 °C) and grease a loaf tin with a little coconut oil or line with baking paper.

2. In a large bowl, thoroughly mix the mashed bananas, coconut oil, maple syrup, and vanilla extract.

3. In another bowl, mix together the oat flour, salt, baking powder, and cinnamon.

4. Add the dry ingredients to the wet ingredients and stir well until everything is well combined. Add the almond milk and stir until the batter is evenly moistened.

5. Fold in the walnuts (if using) and pour the batter into the prepared tin.

6. Bake in the preheated oven for about 50–60 minutes, or until a toothpick comes out clean.

7. Remove from the oven and allow to cool in the pan for at least 10 minutes before slicing.

Nutritional information (per serving)
Calories 220 kcal; Protein 4 g; Fat 10 g;
Sugar 10 g; Carbohydrates 30 g

ENERGY BAR

Easy   **Bars**   **20 Minutes**
+ cooling time   **Vegan**   **Gluten free**

INGREDIENTS

7 oz	dates, pitted and soaked
3.5 oz	almonds
2 oz	walnuts
2 tbsp	chia seeds
2 tbsp	linseed, crushed
¼ tsp	ground cinnamon
¼ tsp	ground ginger
2 tbsp	coconut oil, melted

A pinch of sea salt

Optional: 2 oz dark chocolate (at least 70% cocoa)

PREPARATION

1. Soak the dates in warm water for about 10 minutes, then drain and leave to drain.

2. In the meantime, roughly chop the almonds and walnuts in a food processor and place them in a large bowl.

3. Add the soaked dates to the food processor and process to a smooth paste. Then add to the large bowl containing the nuts.

4. Add the chia seeds, linseed, cinnamon, ginger, and sea salt to the nuts and dates and mix well. Finally, work in the melted coconut oil until you have a sticky mixture.

5. Press the mixture into a baking tin lined with baking paper (approx. 8x8 inches) and smooth out.

6. Melt the dark chocolate over a bain-marie and drizzle over the bar mixture.

7. Place the tin in the fridge for at least 2 hours until the mixture is firm, then cut into bars.

Nutritional information (per bar)
Calories 200 kcal; Protein 5 g; Fat 12 g; Sugar 14 g; Carbohydrates 20 g

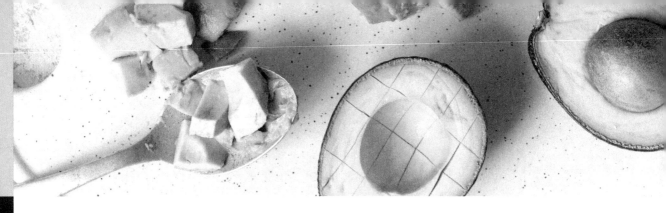

AVOCADO AND TURKEY SANDWICH

Easy · **Portion** · **10 Minutes** · **Gluten-free** · **Nut-free**

INGREDIENTS

2	slices of gluten-free bread
1	ripe avocado, pitted and mashed
3.5 oz	organic turkey breast, sliced
2	thin slices of tomato
1	small red onion, cut into thin rings
1 tbsp	extra virgin olive oil
1 tsp	lemon juice

A handful of rocket

Salt and freshly ground black pepper

A few leaves of fresh basil

PREPARATION

1. Lightly toast the gluten-free bread until it is warm and crispy.

2. Purée the avocado and season with lemon juice, salt and pepper. Spread the avocado cream evenly over the two slices of bread.

3. Place the slices of turkey breast on one of the avocado-covered slices of bread.

4. Spread the rocket, tomato slices, and red onion rings on top and drizzle with olive oil.

5. Sprinkle a few basil leaves over the vegetables and cover with the second slice of bread.

6. Carefully cut the sandwich in half and serve.

Nutritional information (per sandwich)
Calories 350 kcal; Protein 25 g; Fat 20 g;
Sugar 2 g; Carbohydrates 25 g

BAKED VEGETABLE CHIPS

 Easy   Portions   30 Minutes   Vegan   Gluten-free   Nut-free

INGREDIENTS

2   medium sweet potatoes, peeled

2   carrots, peeled

1   beet, peeled

2 tbsp   extra virgin olive oil

½ tsp   ground turmeric

½ tsp   garlic powder

Salt and freshly ground black pepper

PREPARATION

1. Preheat the oven to 360 °F (180 °C). Line a baking tray with baking paper.

2. Cut the sweet potatoes, carrots, and beet into thin slices using a vegetable slicer or food processor.

3. Place the vegetable slices in a large bowl and drizzle with olive oil. Add the sea salt, turmeric, garlic powder, and a grind of black pepper. Mix well so that each vegetable slice is lightly coated with the oil and spices.

4. Place the vegetable slices in a single layer on the prepared baking tray. Ensure the slices do not overlap so they bake evenly and become crispy.

5. Bake the vegetable chips for about 20-25 minutes or until crispy and lightly golden. Halfway through baking, turn the chips once to ensure even browning.

6. Remove the baked vegetable potato chips from the oven and leave to cool for a few minutes before serving.

Nutritional information (per serving)
Calories 120 kcal; Protein 2 g; Fat 7 g;
Sugar 6 g; Carbohydrates 13 g

ENERGY BALLS

Easy

Portions

15 Minutes
+ cooling time

Vegan

Gluten-free

INGREDIENTS

7 oz	Medjool dates, pitted	**1 tbsp**	coconut oil, melted
3.5 oz	rolled oats (glutenfree)	**1 tsp**	cinnamon
2 oz	ground almonds	**½ tsp**	ground ginger
2 tbsp	chia seeds	**2 tbsp**	water (or as required)
2 tbsp	linseed		1 pinch of sea salt

PREPARATION

1. Soak the dates in warm water for about 10 minutes if they are not soft enough. Then drain and pat dry.

2. Pulse the rolled oats, ground almonds, chia seeds, linseed, cinnamon, ginger, and sea salt in a food processor until a coarse mixture is obtained.

3. Add the soaked dates and coconut oil and pulse again until the mixture is well combined and holds together. If the mixture seems too dry, add 1-2 tablespoons of water until it is sticky enough to form balls.

4. Use your hands to form small balls from the mixture. The size can vary as desired, but a size of about one tablespoon per ball is optimal.

5. Arrange the energy balls on a plate or in an airtight box and leave them in the fridge for at least 1 hour before serving.

Nutritional information (per portion/ball)
Calories 100 kcal; Protein 2 g; Fat 5 g;
Sugar 6 g; Carbohydrates 12 g

AVOCADO AND LIME DIP

WITH CHICKPEA CRACKERS

 Medium   **Portions**   **45 Minutes**   **Vegan**   **Gluten-free**   **Nut-free**

INGREDIENTS

2	ripe avocados, pitted and peeled
1	small clove of garlic, finely chopped
2 tbsp	fresh coriander, chopped
1 tbsp	extra virgin olive oil

Juice of 2 limes

Salt and freshly ground black pepper

Optional: 1/4 tsp cayenne pepper

FOR CHICKPEA CRACKERS

7 oz	chickpea flour
1/4 cup	water
2 tbsp	extra virgin olive oil
1 tsp	rosemary, finely chopped
1/4 tsp	garlic powder
1/4 tsp	turmeric powder

Salt

PREPARATION OF THE DIP

1. In a medium bowl, mash the avocados with a fork until the desired consistency is reached.

2. Add the lime juice, chopped garlic, fresh coriander, sea salt, black pepper, and cayenne pepper. Mix everything well until a homogeneous mixture is formed.

3. Finally, stir in the olive oil and taste again to make sure the spices are well-balanced.

4. Transfer the dip to a serving bowl and garnish with additional coriander. Chill in the fridge for a few minutes before serving to intensify the flavors.

PREPARATION OF THE CHICKPEA CRACKERS

5. Preheat the oven to 360 °F (180 °C) and line a baking tray with baking paper.

6. In a bowl, mix the chickpea flour, water, olive oil, sea salt, rosemary, garlic powder, and turmeric powder to form a smooth dough.

7. Roll out the dough between two sheets of baking paper until it is about 3 mm thick. Then, remove the top sheet of paper.

8. Use a knife or pizza roller to cut the dough into cracker sizes, but do not separate them yet.

9. Bake the crackers in the preheated oven for about 20-25 minutes until they are crispy and golden brown.

10. Remove from the oven and allow to cool completely before carefully breaking apart.

Nutritional information (per portion)
Calories 200 kcal; Protein 6 g; Fat 18 g;
Sugar 1 g; Carbohydrates 18 g

INDEX

INDEX

CONCLUSION

THIS COOKBOOK ISN'T JUST ABOUT ALLEVIATING SYMPTOMS

———

It's about enriching your life through conscious eating choices that support your immune system, reduce the risk of chronic disease, and enhance your overall wellness.

As you delve into these pages, allow yourself to experiment and discover what works best for your body. Use this book as your guide to transform your eating habits and foster a life filled with energy and joy. Remember, every meal is an opportunity to treat your body with care and respect. Embrace this chance to nourish yourself in a meaningful way and enjoy the journey towards a healthier, more vibrant you.

FEEDBACK

**THANK YOU VERY MUCH FOR CHOOSING OUR BOOK.
WE HOPE IT WILL BE A GOOD COMPANION FOR YOU AND
THAT YOU HAVE A LOT OF FUN WITH THE RECIPES.**

Feedback and reviews are very important to us. It helps us to understand what we do well and where we can still improve. This allows us to improve the book and make it more useful for you.

If you are satisfied with your purchase, we would therefore very much appreciate a short review on Amazon.

In just 20 seconds, you can give us and other clients great support. You can simply log in to your Amazon account, select this book, and briefly describe what you particularly liked about it.

If you have suggestions for improvement, please scan the QR code. This will take you to a form where you can easily share your suggestions with us.This will help us and future customers enormously.

THANK YOU VERY MUCH FOR YOUR HELP!

RELATED LITERATURE

The Complete Anti-Inflammatory Diet for Beginners
by Dorothy Calimeris and Lulu Cook

The Anti-Inflammatory Diet & Action Plans
by Dorothy Calimeris and Sondi Bruner

Fix It with Food: More Than 125 Recipes to Address Autoimmune Issues and Inflammation
by Michael Symon and Douglas Trattner

The Anti-Inflammation Cookbook: The Delicious Way to Reduce Inflammation and Stay Healthy
by Amanda Haas and Bradly Jacobs

The Inflammation Spectrum: Find Your Food Triggers and Reset Your System
by Will Cole and Eve Adamson

Eat to Beat Disease: The New Science of How Your Body Can Heal Itself
by William W. Li

The Anti-Inflammatory Kitchen Cookbook: More Than 100 Healing, Low-Histamine, Gluten-Free Recipes
by Leslie Langevin

How Not to Die: Discover the Foods Scientifically Proven to Prevent and Reverse Disease
by Michael Greger and Gene Stone

Pure Delicious: More Than 150 Delectable Allergen-Free Recipes
by Heather Christo

Eat to Treat: A Three-Step Plan to Reduce Inflammation, Detoxify Your Life, and Heal Your Body
by Maggie Berghoff

Printed in Great Britain
by Amazon